Praise for *Priestly Presence*

It isn't often that a deeply theological book, rooted in scriptural expertise and imagination, is as accessible and pastoral as is *Priestly Presence: A Church for the World's Sake*. Even as he wades deeply into complex and controversial topics, John Nugent repeatedly makes things understandable to readers at all levels: he breaks things down into practical applications, easy-to-follow categories, and helpful definitions and illustrations. But don't be fooled by its readability—*Priestly Presence* offers a loving but unflinching critique of defective understandings of the church and its mission that permeate nearly all branches of mainstream Christianity. Even more important, Nugent offers a path forward toward a more adequate understanding of the church and its connection to God's kingdom—a map of sorts from which Christians across the traditional divides (e.g., Protestant and Catholic, Reformed and Anabaptist, evangelical and Pentecostal, mainline and marginal) can discern roads worth traveling as they seek to follow The Way of the risen Lord. *Priestly Presence* offers generous amounts of critique and remedy, to the benefit of readers and the entire Christian movement.

> —Michael L. Budde, PhD, professor of Catholic studies
> and political science, Center for World Catholicism
> and Intercultural Theology, DePaul University, and author
> of *Foolishness to Gentiles: Essays on Empire,
> Nationalism, and Discipleship*

The news media surround-sounds us with politics and elections, twenty-four/seven. It has become impossible not to take a stand, not to develop a view, not to form a politics. It's also possible to do all this without solid footings in the gospel or the design of God for his people to be witnesses in the world. John Nugent's very clever and compelling model of the fourfold office of Christ as the Christian posture toward politics will prove to be useful to all who listen carefully. Even more, his five dimensions of a Revised Priestly Model challenged me on every page. May God use this book to revive the church into being what the church is designed by God to be and to become agents of redemption in this world.

> —Scot McKnight, Julius R. Mantey Chair
> of New Testament, Northern Seminary

PRIESTLY PRESENCE

PRIESTLY
PRESENCE

**A Church
for the
World's
Sake**

JOHN C.
NUGENT

FORTRESS PRESS
MINNEAPOLIS

PRIESTLY PRESENCE
A Church for the World's Sake

Library of Congress Cataloging-in-Publication Data

Names: Nugent, John C., author.
Title: Priestly presence : a church for the world's sake / John C. Nugent.
Description: Minneapolis : Fortress Press, [2024] | Includes
    bibliographical references and index.
Identifiers: LCCN 2023045059 (print) | LCCN 2023045060 (ebook) | ISBN
    9781506494043 (print) | ISBN 9781506494050 (ebook)
Subjects: LCSH: Church and the world. | Religion and politics. | Mission of
    the Church. | Clergy--Public relations.
Classification: LCC BR115.W6 N84 2024 (print) | LCC BR115.W6 (ebook) |
    DDC 261/.1--dc23/eng/20231204
LC record available at https://lccn.loc.gov/2023045059
LC ebook record available at https://lccn.loc.gov/2023045060

Cover design: Angela Griner
Cover art: Vector Damask seamless pattern from golden Baroque scrolls by
L_Kramer/iStock

Print ISBN: 978-1-5064-9404-3
eBook ISBN: 978-1-5064-9405-0

I dedicate this book to my friends:
...to my church friends who wrestle with me to discern how best
to live out God's vision for his people,
...to my work friends who walk alongside me each day
as we strive to instill kingdom values into the next generation
of servant leaders,
...to my siblings who encourage my work and challenge
me to write at a level that the widest possible audience
can understand,
...to my wider circle of readers and co-laborers who see
the value of thinking through the important conceptual issues
that inform the day-to-day life of mission-minded Christian
communities in a variety of diverse contexts, and
...to the youth of Delta Community Christian Church,
whose energy and enthusiasm for God's kingdom inspire
me each week to embrace with joy the priestly calling
of God's people for the world's sake.

Contents

Contents

Acknowledgments

I'd like to thank my writing team, which has been instrumental in rounding off some of the rough edges in my grammar, style, and content. I am honored by the time they devoted to helping me see this project to completion. Noteworthy among them are Ryan Apple, Heather Bunce, Dale Burgess, and Branson Parler. I owe each of them a tremendous debt that I am not sure I will ever fully repay.

I also appreciate the work of Ryan Hemmer of Fortress Press who helped me realize that what I had originally envisioned as one book was actually two books. His wise and timely advice is most responsible for the current shape of this project and to some extent *The Fourfold Office of Christ*, which I published in 2024 with Cascade Books.

Finally, I remain grateful to my wife and best friend, Beth. Writing takes a toll on the whole family and Beth has been unwavering in her support. It means the world to me that she sees this work as beneficial enough to God's kingdom mission to devote a decent amount of our family's time and energy to it. I am especially thankful for her assistance in completing this volume's rather lengthy index during a busy season.

Introduction

In the beginning of the twenty-first century, it seemed as if the church had finally conceded the demise of Christendom and began replacing the politics of Washington with the politics of Jesus. Progressives led the charge and evangelicals scrambled to catch up. Racial equality, concern for the poor, elevating the dignity of women—a new social consensus was emerging. And then secularism kicked into overdrive. Long-affirmed conservative views of gender, sex, and marriage (among others) were rapidly overturned. Such swift public change alarmed many evangelicals who feared that public education would only corrupt their youth. Progressives were less rattled since secular values weren't as much at odds with their own.

Then the Trump presidency happened. Conservatives now had a politician who spoke their language, pandered to evangelical concerns (especially on abortion), and promised to protect their values and restore their dignity in the public square. This changed things for many evangelicals. Perhaps they need not abandon politics like the nations, after all—especially since they had a real chance to regain political leverage that they thought they had lost for good. This, in turn, ruffled the feathers of many Christian progressives who now stood to lose ground. A counterattack ensued. Inter-church conflict escalated and many of my pastor friends got caught in the crossfire. Their testimonies are chilling:

- Pastor votes "wrong" way, draws fire from parishioners of opposing political party, nearly loses job, church fractures.
- Elders take unpopular stance on Covid-19, half the church leaves, paid staff resign, congregation falls apart.
- Member objects to a patriotic service, minister pursues a creative solution to maintain unity, elders dismiss minister for being a communist.

- Preacher backs a particular war from the pulpit, elicits mixed responses, eventually resigns, church splits.

Elections, pandemics, patriotism, and war are all public topics of social concern. And the list doesn't stop there. Issues of race, gender, economics, sexual expression, and public health especially threaten the fragile unity that many churches manage to maintain. It's no wonder church membership in America is rapidly declining.[1]

It is tempting to write off such division as a sign of the times. The worse things get in the world, the worse they become in the church. But the church is not simply parroting the partisanship of unbelievers. Its division is rooted in competing convictions about the church's own mandate. Christians disagree profoundly on the precise relationship between church and world, and this disagreement flares up—seemingly with greater intensity—every time a volatile social issue bubbles to the surface of society, like the recent overturning of Roe v. Wade.

I suspect this is because Christians have stopped reflecting critically upon how church and world relate to one another. We assume that Richard Niebuhr's *Christ and Culture* paradigm pretty much settled the matter.[2] Believers no longer debate whether we should get involved in wider social issues. We've all entered the thick of things and are trying, using Niebuhr's language, to "transform culture" for the better without compromising our faith. But this has not united us. We are not involved as kingdom allies fighting together for a common cause. Instead, we find ourselves at odds with one another precisely as we strive to make a positive impact. Christian progressives gravitate toward the political left and Christian conservatives toward the political right. Then all the bad blood between these political factions flows through the veins of our congregations.

In our fumbling attempts to transform this world for the good, we have forsaken our unity, compromised our witness, and dishonored God's name. If Christians truly want to get right with God, we'll need to get right with the world. Only then will we be able to understand what it means for God's

---

1. A Gallop Poll reveals that membership in a church or synagogue has fallen below 50 percent for the first time, dropping from 70 percent to 47 percent from 1992 to 2020. The last decade has seen a 12 percent drop, whereas the previous two decades had dropped only 5 and 6 percent each (https://news.gallup.com/poll/1690/Religion.aspx).

2. H. Richard Niebuhr, *Christ and Culture* (New York: Harper & Row, 1951).

people to exist for the world's sake—not as kings, prophets, or even servants, but as a priestly people, a holy nation. We need to harness the power of priestly presence, and that's what this book is about.

THE POWER OF PRIESTLY PRESENCE

The power of priestly presence is best appreciated in light of the most popular alternatives. So, in chapter 1, I set forth a new typology for relating church and world based on what I call the fourfold office of Christ—prophet, priest, king, and servant.[3] Each of these offices captures a specific way the church might focus its social vision and frame its responsibility to the world. After briefly noting the strengths and weaknesses of each, I argue in chapter 2 that a revised priestly approach should serve as a governing model for the church's posture going forward. This revised approach is grounded in how a variety of Israelite priests served God and people in unique ways, not just the priestly sons of Aaron. Since Israel's priests existed for the sake of Israel as a whole, in chapter 3 I locate the priestly office within God's wider calling for all of Israel. As it turns out, all Israelites served as a priestly people who existed not just for their own kin but for the whole world's sake.

In chapters 4–8, I set forth a fivefold picture of Israelite priesthood that sheds considerable light on how the priestly followers of Christ might live properly in their relationships with God, one another, and the wider world. Priestly aspects I focus on include residence, hospitality, stewardship, witness, and praise. Each chapter begins by detailing the fascinating witness of Israel's priests and then unpacks their relevance to the Christian church and its practical application for all congregations in our own day.

This priestly model offers a creative and compelling vision of a godly people who live each day in every way for the world's sake. If taken seriously, it would help the western church regain its sociopolitical bearings which, in turn, would promote healing and rest for the battle worn body of Christ.

---

3. This book serves as something of a sequel to my book *The Fourfold Office of Christ: A New Typology for Relating Church and World* (Eugene, OR: Cascade Books, 2024). Chapter 1 of this book concisely summarizes what I develop there in depth.

CHAPTER ONE

Beyond Tired Types

THE RISE AND FALL OF *CHRIST AND CULTURE*

As a theology professor who specializes in the church's nature and mission, I appreciate simple frameworks that get students talking about how church and world relate. Typologies perfectly suit this function. They classify a wide variety of phenomena into a small number of general categories. This exposes students to the most common approaches and facilitates discussion of their strengths and weaknesses.

For over seventy years, Richard Niebuhr's *Christ and Culture* has been the go-to resource for facilitating this conversation. It offers a clear and simple typology that maps out five conceptual possibilities: Christ against Culture, Christ of Culture, Christ above Culture, Christ and Culture in Paradox, and Christ Transforming Culture. Like most typologies, one could quibble with Niebuhr's categories, and many have.[1] Still his typology has endured because countless teachers and leaders have found it useful for starting the kinds of conversations that churches need to have.

Lately, however, Niebuhr's categories don't do as much work as they once did. That is because Christians from a variety of backgrounds have taken quite similar stances toward his five categories. Few churches wish to oppose culture wholesale in "Christ against Culture" fashion. Many

---

1. Cf. Glen H. Stassen et al, eds., *Authentic Transformation: A New Vision of Christ and Culture* (Nashville: Abingdon Press, 1996); and Craig Carter, *Rethinking Christ and Culture: A Post-Christendom Perspective* (Grand Rapids: Brazos Press, 2007).

churches strive to present Christ in a form that the wider culture finds agreeable, albeit within limits, and have adopted a soft version of the "Christ of Culture" posture.[2] Most churches renounce top-down coercive leadership over the wider populace in "Christ above Culture" fashion. A soft "Christ and Culture in Paradox" framework is quite common insofar as churches allow their members to embrace different ethical codes in different spheres of their life. Finally, just about every congregation seeks to find creative ways to "transform culture" for the better, which appeared to be Niebuhr's preferred approach.

This growing consensus renders Niebuhr's typology practically obsolete. It gives the false impression that all Christians basically agree on how church and world relate. Yet important differences persist in the twenty-first century, and Niebuhr's familiar categories no longer capture them. If we hope to move beyond rehashing hypothetical possibilities of the past to engaging actual options in the present, we need a fundamentally new typology. That is precisely what I offer in this chapter.

THE FOURFOLD OFFICE OF CHRIST

A well-constructed typology offers simple caricatures of diverse positions that are named in memorable ways. That is partly why I have chosen the familiar threefold office of Christ—prophet, priest, and king—and added a fourth office: servant. You will soon notice, however, that I do not place them in that order. I pair king and servant because they convey opposite positions of power, with kings generally ruling from on high and servants exercising influence from below. I pair prophet and priest because these offices often convey different emphases, with prophets emphasizing social matters and priests emphasizing spiritual matters. I conclude with priest because this book recommends a revised version of the priestly type as the most biblical and beneficial approach. It holds the most promise for helping the church carry out its divine calling for the sake of the world.

For the remainder of this chapter, I introduce each type with a simple overview, as if written from the perspective of a church that espouses it. I

---

2. Consider how quickly Christians have embraced wider cultural views on marriage, divorce, money, entertainment, guns, drugs, and politics—whether in the forms championed by the left or the right.

frame it as an enthusiastic invitation to join such a church (e.g., a "prophetic church" or a "servant church"). Think of each introduction as a two-minute promo that encapsulates the position with memorable simplicity. Then I evaluate the strengths and weaknesses of each one conceptually, biblically, and practically. This prepares us to appreciate the revised priestly approach recommended in this book.

The Kingly Church

Welcome to the Kingly Church!

The powers of this world need guidance. They rule in ignorance because they're oblivious to what really makes for human thriving. Though created in God's image, they fail to reflect his glory as they exercise dominion over creation. This is not entirely their fault: sin has so clouded our vision and fractured the divine image in us all that we fail to see and reflect God's good intentions for the world. The broken and blinded powers cannot help but fumble around in the dark until someone shows them the light.

As sons and daughters of the Eternal King, the church of God must rise up and accept this charge. Through Christ we are being renewed in the image of the Creator.[3] We have been raised up and seated with him in heavenly places.[4] We alone possess the vantage point to see through the eyes of the Creator and mirror his glory to all creation. We must not neglect our royal mandate. It is laid out clearly at the beginning of the Bible story and realized fully at the end:

> Then God said, "Let us make humankind *in our image*, according to our likeness; and *let them have dominion* over the fish of the sea, and over the birds of the air, and over the cattle, and over all the wild animals of the earth, and over every creeping thing that creeps upon the earth." (Gen 1:26)

> Jesus said to them, "Truly I tell you, at the renewal of all things, when the Son of Man is seated on the throne of his glory, *you who have followed*

---

3. Col 3:10.
4. Eph 2:6.

> me will also sit on twelve thrones, judging the twelve tribes of Israel." (Matt 19:28)

> The saying is sure: If we have died with him, we will also live with him; if we endure, *we will also reign with him.* (2 Tim 2:11–12)

> To everyone who conquers and continues to do my works to the end, *I will give authority over the nations.* (Rev 2:26)

> You have made them to be a kingdom and priests serving our God, and *they will reign on earth.* (Rev 5:10)

> And there will be no more night; they need no light of lamp or sun, for the Lord God will be their light, and *they will reign forever and ever.* (Rev 22:5)

Our exalted status was made possible by Christ. Where Israel failed to recover God's image, Jesus succeeded—and he did so on our behalf. The good news is that we can die to our old selves and be raised anew with Christ and renewed in the image of our King.[5] What Adam and Eve lost on behalf of all humanity, Christ regained once and for all.

We must now fulfill our mandate to reflect his glory and exercise godly dominion throughout all creation. As restored icons of the divine, only we are prepared and positioned to show this world what true dominion looks like. As sons and daughters of the king, it is our birthright, our regal responsibility.

Assessing the Kingly Church

The Kingly Church has a lot going for it. It builds on the work of noteworthy Bible scholars like N. T. Wright, arguably the most influential Christian thinker of the twenty-first century.[6] Tim Mackie, with his informative, well-produced, and easily accessible Bible Project videos, has popularized it.[7] It locates the

---

5. Col 3:10.

6. N. T. Wright, *After You Believe: Why Christian Character Matters* (New York: Harper One, 2010). Cf. also G. K. Beale, *The Temple and the Church's Mission: A Biblical Theology of the Dwelling Place of God* (Downers Grove, IL: InterVarsity Press, 2004); and John H. Walton, *Genesis*, NIV Application Commentary (Grand Rapids: Eerdmans, 2001).

7. See the Bible Project's "Image of God"–themed video at https://bibleproject.com/explore/themes.

church's posture within a coherent telling of the full Bible story, from Genesis to Revelation. When combined with the priestly image, it offers a rich and compelling account of God's redemption of all creation, the central work of Christ, and the pivotal role of the church in God's global mission.

Still, the kingly image suffers some glaring weaknesses. Foremost among them is Scripture's devastating critique of royal power. The earth's first rulers spread oppression and violence throughout the earth.[8] God therefore instructs his chosen people in Torah to steer clear of kingship like the nations. When Israel embraces worldly kingship anyway, God decries their rebellion and waits patiently as the entire project crumbles under the weight of its inadequacies.[9] Through the prophet Isaiah, God then reframes Israel's future in terms of the unimpressive work of a lowly servant—an image that refers to both the people of God and their coming Savior.[10]

Of all the diverse Old Testament images, the New Testament writers follow Jesus in framing his reign in terms of Isaiah's servant. Jesus rejected all opportunities and temptations to wield kingly power and instructed his wannabe kingly followers to spurn pagan notions of ruling and embrace his missional posture of service (Mark 10:42–45).[11] Indeed, nothing in the actions of Jesus or his followers suggests that the kingly image provided any inspiration for how they engaged the world.

Why then do prominent Christian influencers gravitate toward it? They believe it enjoys considerable biblical support. Numerous passages scattered throughout the Bible refer to God's people using royal imagery. Yet when read in context, they do not commend the royal posture as one that Israel or the church should take toward the world. Some depict the coming reversal of Israel's lowly downtrodden status using royal imagery.[12] Others note that God will someday confer a glorious kingdom upon his people.[13] Still others anticipate the followers of Jesus reigning with him.[14]

Yet one must be careful not to approach these passages with an over-realized eschatology. Most of them describe the state of God's chosen people

---

8. See my commentary on Gen 4:23–24, 6:1–4, and 11:1–9 in Nugent, *Genesis 1–11*, The Polis Bible Commentary (La Vista, NE: Urban Loft Publishers, 2018).

9. 1 Sam 8:4–9 and Hos 13:11.

10. Isa 42:1–4; 49:1–6; 50:4–7; and 52:13–53:12.

11. See Matt 4:1–11; John 6:15; Acts 1:6; and John 18:33–37.

12. E.g., Obad 21; Isa 14:2; and 45:14.

13. E.g., Dan 7:27.

14. E.g., Matt 19:28; 2 Tim 2:12; Rev 2:26–27; 5:10; 20:6; and 22:5.

when God's kingdom is filled to its fullest—after Christ returns. At that time, believers will indeed reign with Christ, whatever that looks like. Until then, we serve. And we know what that looks like: it's like Jesus who walked among us and set an example for us to follow. We are not called to rule through the power of servanthood, but to serve as lowly, Spirit-empowered witnesses to God's reign.

Key to the kingly image's biblical support is Genesis 1–3. It depicts humans as divine image bearers on whom God confers dominion over the earth. Lamentably, according to the kingly narrative, humans lost God's image by striving to be more like him in forbidden ways (the fall). Israel was supposed to recover that image through exemplary obedience but fell short. Where Israel failed, Christ succeeded. And having been remade in his image, Jesus's followers may now rightfully reclaim our dominion mandate.

This interpretation is riddled with shortcomings. Scripture says that God made all humans in his image and not just the chosen people. The Bible never indicates that humanity as a whole lost the divine image or the dominion mandate on account of sin. Furthermore, Genesis 12 through Malachi makes no mention whatsoever of the divine image trope. It plays no part in Israel's calling or legacy as God's people. This language remains conspicuously absent in the ministry of Jesus and the apostles. We only see a couple of Pauline passages that describe Christian salvation in terms of being remade in the image of Christ, yet with no connection to the dominion mandate.[15]

As the Bible story unfolds from Genesis 1, all humans remain divine image bearers who exercise dominion over nonhuman creation—even after the flood according to Genesis 9:6. God's people should indeed exemplify what this looks like, but that doesn't make it more our responsibility than anyone else's. Nor does it entitle any person or group, let alone God's people, to exercise dominion over others. The dominion mandate always was—and still remains—a universal human responsibility over nonhuman creation. Dominion departs from divine intent when it devolves into humans seeking power and authority over other humans, even for their own good. Worldly rulers do precisely this, and Jesus forbids his people from following their lead (Luke 22:25–26).

---

15. 2 Cor 3:18 and Col 3:10.

Weaknesses like these, I suspect, lead scholars to soften the kingly image by combining it with the priestly image. They do so, first of all, by interpreting the earliest dominion-bearing humans in Genesis 1–3 as priests and the garden of Eden as a temple. I critique the weakness of this interpretation elsewhere,[16] but suffice it to say the text simply doesn't say so without excessive intertextual wrangling. It relies upon numerous inferences and weak parallels. Proponents of the Kingly Church then jump to Exodus 19:6, where God refers to Israel as a "kingdom of priests." In their view, God here confers upon Israel the dual role of *kings* and *priests*.[17] But the text does not say that. God does not refer to the Israelites as a "kingdom of priests *and* kings" but a "kingdom of priests." This phrase speaks only of their priestly role. We find the same priestly emphasis in 1 Peter 2:5–9, which appropriates the Exodus 19 image with no mention of the ruling function of God's people. In fact, Scripture combines the image of priests with the act of reigning only in the book of Revelation. There the priestly function pertains to the current age and the royal function awaits a future time, after Christ's return.[18]

The Kingly Church is not altogether without merit. It forefronts several issues that God's people must take seriously. It strives to locate the posture of the church in a coherent telling of the full Bible story. This effort is crucial even if the telling it offers comes up short. By beginning in Genesis 1, the Kingly Church situates the church's calling within God's original intentions for creation. That enables this view to take seriously the full range of sin's devastating consequences—not just the vertical, spiritual, or individual dimensions. In this sense, the kingly approach affirms creation and does not absolve believers of the ecological responsibility inherent in being good humans. Both the laws of Torah and the theology of the apostle Paul affirm that responsibility.[19] The Kingly Church type shines when it points Christians toward a grander theology than that which focuses exclusively on our relationship with God and fellow believers. But it simply carries too much baggage to serve as a governing image for the Church's relationship to the world.

---

16. Nugent, *Genesis 1–11*, 34–38; and Nugent, *Fourfold Office of Christ*, ch. 3.

17. Wright, *After You Believe*, 80.

18. Rev 5:10 and 20:6. Revelation 1:6 also has priest and dominion language, but it assigns priestly service to the church and dominion to God the Father or perhaps Jesus Christ.

19. Rom 8:18–24.

The Servant Church

Welcome to the Servant Church!

The powers of this world leave much to be done. Government programs and wealthy philanthropists simply aren't enough to meet this world's needs. Far too many people fall through the cracks—people whom God deeply loves: the destitute, the forgotten, the outcast. The marginalized of this world desperately need to experience the hands and feet of Jesus, actively serving where and when no one else will.

Followers of Jesus must take up the towel and basin and join him in washing the feet of others. As he is in this world, so must we be.[20] We are his bodily presence in and for this world until he returns. So we constantly remind one another to do the kinds of things Jesus did when he walked among us—touching the lepers, healing the sick, feeding the hungry, and raising the lowly. The Scriptures make this crystal clear:

> Whoever wishes to be great among you must be your servant, and whoever wishes to be first among you must be your slave; just as the Son of Man came not to be served but to serve, and to give his life a ransom for many. (Matt 20:26–28)

> Then the righteous will answer him, "Lord, when was it that we saw you hungry and gave you food, or thirsty and gave you something to drink? And when was it that we saw you a stranger and welcomed you, or naked and gave you clothing? And when was it that we saw you sick or in prison and visited you?" And the king will answer them, "Truly I tell you, just as you did it to one of the least of these who are members of my family, you did it to me." (Matt 25:37–40)

> After he had washed their feet, had put on his robe, and had returned to the table, he said to them, "Do you know what I have done to you? You call me Teacher and Lord—and you are right, for that is what I am. So if I, your Lord and Teacher, have washed your feet, you also ought to wash one another's feet. For I have set you an example, that you also should do as I have done to you." (John 13:12–15)

---

20. 1 John 4:17.

Religion that is pure and undefiled before God, the Father, is this: to care for orphans and widows in their distress, and to keep oneself unstained by the world. (Jas 1:27)

Such acts of kindness should not be reduced to occasional service projects. They are the gospel made visible in world history. In Luke 4, Jesus launched his ministry on the platform of Isaiah 61: "The Spirit of the Lord is upon me, because he has anointed me to bring good news to the poor. He has sent me to proclaim release to the captives and recovery of sight to the blind, to let the oppressed go free, to proclaim the year of the Lord's favor."[21] And he has called us to continue this ministry. We must therefore discern where God is working and join him. We must serve this world at its point of need, whether that means ladling soup, housing refugees, befriending widows, visiting prisoners, or speaking out for the voiceless.

The church exists *for the world* or not at all. As God so loves the world, so must we!

Assessing the Servant Church

Where the kingly model is weak, the servant model is strong.[22] Since the notion of humans exercising top-down authority fares poorly in Scripture, the best versions of the Kingly Church clarify that any dominion believers wield must be exercised by way of service, imitating the way of Jesus.[23] The Servant Church simply eliminates the middle man by removing kingly language from the equation. Jesus took the posture of a servant and called his followers to do the same.[24] There is nothing ambiguous or purely futuristic about this calling. It is reinforced by numerous passages that instruct God's people to love radically, care for "the least of these," and place others' needs before their

---

21. Luke 4:18–19 echoes Isaiah 61:1–2.

22. The "servant" image represented by this position should not be confused with voiceless, choiceless, demeaning servitude like that of chattel slavery or sex trafficking. Rather it is characterized by cheerful, willful, self-giving service for the good of others. Believers serve not out of compulsion but out of love.

23. Matthew W. Bates. *The Gospel Precisely: Surprisingly Good News about Jesus Christ the King* (RENEW.org, 2020), 43.

24. Matt 20:26; 23:11; Mark 10:43; Luke 22:26; and John 13:3–17.

own.[25] The Servant Church fulfills the Servant Songs of Isaiah by continuing the "suffering servant" mission of Christ (1 Pet 2:21–25).[26] Most importantly, the church's servant posture is grounded in the fact that the church exists fundamentally *for* the world. Because God exists for the world, he has called into existence a people who serve him by also existing for the world.[27]

Though the Servant Church surpasses the Kingly Church in many regards, it doesn't quite capture how God has called his people to exist for this world. Most passages cited in its favor aren't even about the church's relationship to the world. Servant passages in the New Testament focus on God's people serving God, Christ, fellow believers, God's Word, and the gospel.[28] The only passage using "servant" language in relation to the wider world is Mark 9:35, which calls kingdom citizens to be servants "of all." Yet this passage fails to specify what such service entails. Is it benevolence? Some sort of chaplaincy? Evangelism? We cannot be sure. Indeed, prominent scholars have observed that the posture of servant to the world enjoys little biblical support.[29]

The Parable of the Sheep and Goats in Matthew 25 is routinely misread in support of the Servant Church. When Jesus says that whatever we have done or left undone for the "least of these" we have done or left undone for him, he is not talking about Christian service to unbelievers. He specifies in verse 40 that he is talking about the least of the members of his family

---

25. E.g., Matt 22:36–40; 25:34–36; and Phil 2:5–11. See Barbara DeGrote Sorensen and David Allen, *Let the Servant Church Arise!* (Minneapolis: Augsburg Fortress Press, 2003), 20–24.

26. Matthew S. Harmon, *The Servant of the Lord and His Servant People: Tracing a Biblical Theme Through the Canon* (Downers Grove, IL: InterVarsity Press, 2020), ch. 6–7. Other passages connecting the church to Christ's suffering servant posture include Rom 6:6–11; 2 Cor 1:5–6; 2 Cor 4:8–11; Phil 3:10–11; Col 1:24; and 1 Pet 3:14–18; 4:1–2, 12–16.

27. Karl Barth develops this theme at length in *Church Dogmatics* IV.3.2, translated by Geoffrey W. Bromiley (Edinburgh: T and T Clark, 1962), § 72, 2, pp. 762–795.

28. For service to God, see Matt 4:10 // Luke 4:8; Matt 6:24 // Luke 16:13; Luke 1:38–74; Acts 4:29; 20:19; Rom 1:9; 12:11; 14:4; 1 Cor 3:5, 9; 4:1; 2 Cor 6:4; Eph 6:7; 1 Thess 1:9; 2 Tim 2:24; Titus 1:1; Jas 1:1; 1 Pet 2:16; Rev 1:1, 6; 2:19–20; 5:10; 7:3; 19:5, 10; 22:3, 6. For service to Christ, see John 12:26; Rom 1:1; 14:8; Gal 1:10; Phil 1:1; Col 1:7; 3:24; 4:7, 12; 1 Tim 4:6; Jas 1:1; 2 Pet 1:1; Jude 1. For service to fellow believers, see Matt 20:26 // Matt 23:11 // Mark 10:43 // Luke 22:26; Rom 15:27; 1 Cor 16:15–16; 2 Cor 8:23; 11:8; Phil 2:30; 1 Tim 3:10, 13; 1 Tim 6:2; Phlm 13; Heb 6:10; 1 Pet 1:12; 1 Pet 4:10–11. For service to the gospel or word, see Luke 1:2; Acts 6:4; Rom 15:16; Eph 3:7; Phil 2:22; Col 1:23, 25; and 1 Tim 1:12.

29. E.g., Avery Cardinal Dulles, *Models of Church*, expanded ed. (New York: Image Books, 2002), ch. 6; Gerhard Lohfink, *Jesus and Community: The Social Dimension of Christian Faith* (Philadelphia: Fortress, 1984), 106–115.

("brothers" in Greek). He was likely referring to early Christian apostles and evangelists whom he tasked with taking the gospel from town to town. Many of them depended upon receptive listeners to provide their food, clothing, and lodging—especially when hostile authorities placed them in prison on account of the gospel. Similarly, the overwhelming majority of love passages in Scripture speak to love for God or fellow believers.[30] Even the widows and orphans for which God holds his people responsible are likely members of the kingdom community.[31]

None of this means that Christians should not render loving, compassionate service to needy unbelievers in their community and throughout the world. Holistic evangelism will meet people at their point of need both spiritually and physically.[32] It should simply give us pause before attributing wider world service to every Bible passage commending love and concern for the poor and needy.

Dietrich Bonhoeffer saw deeper problems with the Servant Church model. He insisted that the church has no business trying to solve the world's problems, since God's word does not offer the solution humans think they need. God offers redemption, not solutions.[33] Christ offers a kingdom that transcends human problems and, in so doing, resolves them truly and fully. As such, according to Bonhoeffer, the church's relationship to the world derives exclusively from the gospel of Jesus Christ. He concludes, "The church's message to the world is the word about the coming of God in the flesh, about God's love for the world in the sending of God's Son, about God's judgment on unbelief. The church's message is the call to turn around, to believe in God's love in Christ, to prepare for the second coming of Christ, the coming kingdom of God. It is thus the word of redemption for all people."[34]

If Bonhoeffer is right, then the New Testament's failure to address all the world's social problems by way of a Servant Church is not a failure at all but an accurate reflection of God's priorities for his people. The early church was

---

30. Lohfink, *Jesus and Community,* 110.

31. Acts 6:1–4; 1 Tim 5:3–10; and even Jas 1:27 when read in the context of Jas 2.

32. Ronald J. Sider, Philip N. Olson, and Heidi Rolland Unruh, *Churches that Make a Difference: Reaching Your Community with Good News and Good Works* (Grand Rapids: Baker Books, 2002).

33. Dietrich Bonhoeffer, *Ethics,* Dietrich Bonhoeffer Works 6 (Minneapolis: Fortress Press, 2005), 354.

34. Bonhoeffer, *Ethics,* 356.

so completely enraptured by the new order of God's kingdom that they were not lured into serving the old orders that God's kingdom was replacing. First century believers did care about social concerns, but their way of caring for them centered on the alternative social order of God's kingdom represented by the church.

Still, the Servant Church may be able to answer Bonhoeffer's concern. If the church's calling revolves around proclaiming and bearing witness to Christ's kingdom work, then one need only demonstrate that meeting the world's needs in Servant Church fashion meets the criteria of kingdom work. Reggie McNeal takes this approach.[35] He associates kingdom work with any action that brings the present world into closer alignment with the abundant life of the world to come. In Jesus's day, that meant the lame walking, the blind seeing, and lepers being made whole. Today, it looks like kids learning to read, the unemployed finding jobs, the uninsured acquiring good health care, and homeless people finding homes.[36] Wherever God's will for human thriving in creation is realized, the kingdom breaks through.[37]

Unfortunately, this approach reflects kingdom confusion. McNeal has identified some key aspects of the kingdom, extracted them from the Bible story, inserted them into the world's project of perpetual human progress, and then equated that project with God's kingdom. But the Bible story does not portray God setting apart a people who seek out the world's brokenness and then try to fix it using divine revelation. That was not Israel's task, not Jesus's task, and certainly not that of the early church.[38] In McNeal's vision, humans bring the kingdom through good works. In Scripture, God brings the kingdom through Christ, and we accept it as a gift. For McNeal, the church excels when it improves the old order that is passing away. In Scripture, the church excels when it bears witness to Christ's new order that has already begun to replace the old one. Karl Barth correctly insisted that the church cannot lift a finger to bring God's kingdom, but we can and must serve as witnesses to God's work in Christ—a significant and demanding task on its own.[39]

---

35. Reggie McNeal, *Kingdom Come: Why We Must Give up Our Obsession with Fixing the Church—and What We Should Do Instead* (Carol Stream, IL: Tyndale Publishers, 2015).

36. McNeal, *Kingdom Come*, 11.

37. McNeal, *Kingdom Come*, 25.

38. This proposal is so deeply flawed that I dedicated an entire book to dismantling it. Cf. John C. Nugent, *Endangered Gospel: How Fixing the World Is Killing the Church* (Eugene, OR: Cascade Books), 2016.

39. Barth, CD IV.3.2, § 72, 4, p. 835.

And so, the Servant Church must be careful. The church's existence for the world is, indeed, its highest calling. But it exists only by God's appointment. It must render the service demanded by its one and only Lord. When we begin with human perspectives on how to provide the needs of the world, we risk becoming servants of lame duck kingdoms that stand under God's judgment. Instead, we must be servants of God and the new world he has assigned to us. Jesus was surely right. We cannot serve two masters. We will inevitably love the one and despise the other.[40] Let the Servant Church find creative ways to serve the world that place our love for God on full display through our love for one another. That way, the world may receive both a respite from old world suffering and an invitation to new world joy in fellowship. I'm not suggesting we must preach to people before we can feed them. But we should display the lordship of Jesus Christ in the way we share food. Are we just dishing out meals or are we welcoming the hungry to a kingdom banquet? At this table, Christ is the head, sinners are welcome, children are cherished, women are honored, the great are least, the lowly are exalted, and we all take turns washing each other's feet.

The Prophetic Church

Welcome to the Prophetic Church!

The powers of this world are corrupt. They are driven by greed and they serve only those who pad their pockets, place them in office, and keep them there. But it's not just the politicians. It's corporations, financiers, news media, the entire establishment through and through. And they will continue to monopolize the wealth of our small towns and big cities until someone exposes them for the ruthless predators they are.

God's people must find our prophetic voice. We must unite and speak truth to power. Our preachers give it to us straight—capturing the fiery spirit of eighth-century prophets like Isaiah, Micah, Hosea and, above all, Amos. These men of old held nothing back. They decried all forms of injustice and exposed the privileged few who amassed power, hoarded wealth, and crushed the vulnerable beneath them. No corrupt leader escaped their gaze, whether king, prince, judge, or prophet.

---

40. Matt 6:24.

Hear this, O priests! Give heed, O house of Israel!
Listen, O house of the king! For the judgment pertains to you.
(Hos 5:1)

Take away from me the noise of your songs;
I will not listen to the melody of your harps.
But let justice roll down like waters,
And righteousness like an everflowing stream. (Amos 5:23–24)

Wash yourselves; make yourselves clean;
remove the evil of your doings from before my eyes;
cease to do evil, learn to do good;
seek justice, rescue the oppressed,
defend the orphan, plead for the widow. (Isa 1:16–17)

He has told you, O mortal, what is good;
and what does the LORD require of you
but to do justice, and to love kindness,
and to walk humbly with your God? (Micah 6:8)

Jesus came to fulfill the hope of these prophets. He proclaimed the good news of God's kingdom—a kingdom in which the high and mighty are brought low, the lowly and meek are raised up, and the kingdoms of this world crumble before the kingdom of God. How hard it is for the rich to enter this kingdom! John the Baptist, the greatest old covenant prophet, blazed the trail before us, crying, "Repent, for the kingdom of heaven has come near!"[41] He challenged the crowds to share their resources with those who lacked. He warned public servants to stop fleecing the people and be content with their wages.[42] He publicly shamed King Herod for presuming he could marry whomever he wished.[43]

Like the baptizer, we must stand ready to speak up when our time comes. When rights are infringed, we take to the streets with our signs and our megaphones. As key verdicts are rendered, we gather on court steps in solidarity and in prayer. Our quips and memes populate the Twittersphere and

41. Matt 3:2.
42. Luke 3:10–14.
43. Mark 6:17–18.

dominate the feeds on Instagram and Facebook. When election days approach and social unrest bubbles over, we are poised for action. We were called for such times as these.

God's voice will be heard! It must be heard—for the sake of this broken world. And if we don't answer this prophetic calling, our silence will condemn us. Corrupt powers beware! Complicit Christians, wake up! The kingdom of God is at hand![44]

Assessing the Prophetic Church

When God gives a word to his people, they dare not keep it to themselves. The prophet Amos put it this way, "Surely the Lord GOD does nothing, without revealing his secret to his servants the prophets. The lion has roared; who will not fear? The Lord GOD has spoken; who can but prophesy?"[45] This remains true even when God's word brings ridicule and persecution. Jeremiah, the tormented prophet, referred to God's word as "a burning fire" shut up within his bones. Try as he may, he could not hold it in.[46] Moses wished that all of God's people were prophets, and the prophet Joel foresaw a day when God fulfills that wish.[47] The apostle Peter announced the dawn of that day on the festival of Pentecost, shortly after Jesus ascended and poured his Spirit upon the church.[48] Nothing could be more biblical than the church boldly proclaiming God's word to the world. What is more, Israel's prophets exemplified the need to unite the vertical and horizontal demands of God's word. It's not enough to tell unbelievers how to get right with God, we must implore the world to pursue justice and do right by the poor, marginalized,

---

44. Though this depiction of the Prophetic Church is a caricature, some recent books that emphasize the church's prophetic role in various ways include Walter Brueggemann, *The Prophetic Imagination*, 2nd ed. (Minneapolis: Fortress Press, 2001); Mary Doak, *A Prophetic, Public Church: Witness to Hope Amid the Global Crises of the Twenty-First Century* (Collegeville, MN: Liturgical Press, 2020); Luke Timothy Johnson, *Prophetic Jesus, Prophetic Church: The Challenge of Luke-Acts to Contemporary Christians* (Grand Rapids, MI: Eerdmans, 2011); Eric Mason, *Woke Church: An Urgent Call for Christians in America to Confront Racism and Injustice* (Chicago: Moody Publishers, 2018); and Miroslav Volf, *A Public Faith: How Followers of Christ Should Serve the Common Good* (Grand Rapids, MI: Brazos, 2011).

45. Amos 3:7–8.

46. Jer 20:9.

47. Num 11:29 and Joel 2:28–29.

48. Acts 2:14–21.

and oppressed. Uniting the social and spiritual dimensions of the gospel proved to be one of the great theological accomplishments of the twentieth century. We should commend the Prophetic Church for keeping them united in the church's witness to the world.

Like the Kingly and Servant churches, however, the Prophetic Church fails to capture God's vision for how his people ought to relate to the world. Why? For starters, prophecy is first and foremost an in-house practice according to Scripture. Almost without exception, Old Testament prophets spoke truth to fellow Israelites and their leaders. Every prophetic book was written to God's people because all the oracles they contain were delivered to the Israelites. Even when the prophets spoke about and against other nations, they crafted those messages for Israel and delivered them to God's people alone.[49] God's future plans for the nations served to warn his chosen people against allying with those nations. They also encouraged God's people that though these nations appear to be in control of world history, they are not. Each, in turn, will fall before the God of Israel on account of the injustices they have committed.

This pattern continues in the New Testament. In 1 Corinthians, Paul discusses the nature of prophecy more than any other letter. He informs believers in Corinth that prophecy is meant to build up the church.[50] He specifies that "prophecy is not for unbelievers but for believers."[51] This assertion is rooted in the difference between how believers should relate to those inside and outside of the church. "For what have I to do with judging those outside?" Paul asks rhetorically. "Is it not those who are inside that you are to judge?"[52] His approach is not novel. It's the approach taken by a long line of Israelite prophets.

Why not prophesy to unbelievers? What harm could come from speaking truth to pagan powers? Irreparable harm might come! For starters, believers and unbelievers follow different standards. Israelite prophets speak to fellow Israelites and their rulers because God called all of Israel to follow Torah, including their kings.[53] When Israel doesn't follow Torah, their witness falters. God then disciplines them because his mission to the nations depends on his people's faithfulness. Furthermore, God has promised to bless his people and

---

49. E.g., Obadiah, Nahum, Isaiah 10–25, Jeremiah 46–51, and Ezekiel 25–32.

50. 1 Cor 14:3–4.

51. 1 Cor 14:22. Though Paul points out vv. 24–25 that unbelievers who enter the assembly of believers may be convicted by the prophetic word being spoken among us and will conclude that God is with us.

52. 1 Cor 5:12.

53. Deut 17:18–19.

empower them to live out his vision for human thriving. Without God's provision, they cannot meet God's standards. Knowing this, God gave Israel his Torah, his prophets, his priests, his blessing on their agricultural endeavors, his protection from external foes, and his tabernacling presence. The same goes for the church. God has given us the example of Jesus, the company of fellow believers, the regeneration of baptism, the light of Scripture, and the empowerment of his Holy Spirit. Without these resources, we cannot even begin to live out God's kingdom vision.

God's people presume much when we expect unbelievers to obey God's vision without such provision. When we do so, the unbelieving world experiences God's gracious word as law and not gift. It is a rod we strike them with and not abundant life we invite them to. God's people do, in fact, have a word to proclaim to the world. We must proclaim God's offer to enter the kingdom through Jesus Christ. We are right to inform unbelievers that their lives must change if they hope to enter that kingdom, but we dare not ask them to die to their old lives apart from inviting them into the new and abundant life we share in Christ. As faith without works is dead, requiring works without offering faith is death dealing. I suspect this is why Paul insisted that believers have no business judging unbelievers. God will judge them in due time; we must proclaim Christ to them. Apart from Christ they cannot and will not withstand divine judgment.

"Wait a second," you may be thinking. "Didn't several Old Testament prophets speak to unbelievers?" What about Joseph, Moses, Jonah, Elijah, Elisha, and Daniel? Or perhaps John the Baptist, Jesus, or Paul in the New Testament? These prophets appear to be exceptions to the general rule, but they are not as exceptional as it may seem. Neither Joseph, Moses, Jonah, nor Daniel sought to speak truth to the powers of their day so as to decry their social injustices. Joseph was hauled before Pharaoh to interpret a dream and said nothing about the king's injustices. Both Jonah and Moses did their best to avoid speaking to foreign rulers, but God overwhelmed their reticence with miraculous displays of divine power. Even so, their messages focused on God's coming judgment. Jonah briefly proclaimed Nineveh's impending doom and then promptly departed. Moses made God's request that Pharaoh let his people go and then warned of divine judgment when he wouldn't. Neither prophet said anything about how these kings lorded over their own people. We can say the same of Elijah and Elisha. They relayed messages to a pagan king concerning who would succeed him, but that's it. These instances show only that God sometimes uses prophets to convey a specific message to ruling powers about the future. None of them played the part that the Prophetic Church wishes to play.

Jesus and Paul in the New Testament continue this pattern. They sometimes speak with foreign powers but never criticize their social injustices. John the Baptist alone gives moral censure to unbelieving powers. He has no qualms telling soldiers, presumably Roman, how to do their job better.[54] But they came to him and asked how they might repent in preparation for the coming kingdom. The baptizer's answer was thus gospel proclamation. John's criticism of King Herod's marital unfaithfulness, on the other hand, appears to have been unsolicited. Yet Herod wasn't a typical pagan ruler.[55] He was partly Jewish, he was marrying a woman of Jewish descent, he presented himself as a Jewish sympathizer, he ruled over mostly Jewish territory, he considered himself a righteous and holy man, and he enjoyed listening to John's teaching.[56] For all these reasons, John's criticism of Herod more closely resembles in-house prophetic critique.

In today's religious culture, people commonly hail Christians who confront secular authorities as prophets. Such political activism, truthful as it may be in content, does not bear the insignia of biblical prophecy. At its best it adds to wider society's ever-flowing stream of public criticism, which may or may not convince the powers to amend their wicked ways. At its worst it distorts the world's perception of the church and inhibits their ability to see the gospel as a gift.

The Priestly Church

Welcome to the Priestly Church!

The powers of this world may be able to keep chaos and violence in check for a while, but they cannot mediate a lasting peace between humans and God or humans and one another. They cannot atone for the disastrous consequences of sin. They can put food on the plate, cops on the street, and charitable policies into law. But only Christ truly saves and makes us whole. Christ alone serves as

---

54. Luke 3:14. There's also an outside chance these soldiers were actually Jewish.

55. See Bruce Chilton, *The Herods: Murder, Politics, and the Art of Succession* (Minneapolis, MN: Fortress Press, 2021).

56. Mark 6:20.

the Mediator in whom salvation may be found. Christ did not write his saving work in the clouds or etch it into cliffs. He wrote it in the hearts of his people. The lost and dying world will only know if someone shows and tells them.

God's priestly people are responsible for displaying and proclaiming Christ—the ultimate High Priest of our salvation. Christ sent us into this world to make himself known. Our priestly service derives entirely from that of Christ. We do not make people right; God accomplished that through Jesus. We serve the world best by proclaiming his sacrifice for them, baptizing people into Christ, and participating in that sacrifice together in the breaking of bread. God has made us a priestly nation for the sake of all nations in this world. This calling spans the entirety of Scripture.

> I will make of you a great nation, and I will bless you, and make your name great, so that you will be a blessing. I will bless those who bless you, and the one who curses you I will curse; and in you all the families of the earth shall be blessed. (Gen 12:2–3)

> If you obey my voice and keep my covenant, you shall be my treasured possession out of all the peoples. Indeed, the whole earth is mine, but you shall be for me a priestly kingdom and a holy nation. (Exod 19:5–6)

> You shall be called priests of the LORD, you shall be named ministers of our God; you shall enjoy the wealth of the nations, and in their riches you shall glory. (Isa 61:6)

> Present your bodies as a living sacrifice, holy and acceptable to God, which is your spiritual worship. Do not be conformed to this world, but be transformed by the renewing of your minds, so that you may discern what is the will of God—what is good and acceptable and perfect. (Rom 12:1–2)

> Come to him, a living stone, though rejected by mortals yet chosen and precious in God's sight, and like living stones, let yourselves be built into a spiritual house, to be a holy priesthood, to offer spiritual sacrifices acceptable to God through Jesus Christ. (1 Pet 2:4–5)

> To him who loves us and freed us from our sins by his blood, and made us to be a kingdom, priests serving his God and Father, to him be glory and dominion forever and ever. (Rev 1:5–6)

God conferred our priestly calling upon us through Christ. We are not holy, but God has made us stewards of his holiness. We are not worthy, but God has cleansed us by the blood of the Lamb. We cannot mediate between God and humanity, but we can lead others to the one Mediator who can. We serve God in word and sacrament. We offer ourselves to God and this world in worship, praise, blessing, and instruction.

Our most profound priestly responsibility is to proclaim Christ, who gave his own life as an atoning sacrifice not just for our sins but for all the sins of the world.[57]

Assessing the Priestly Church

The priestly model of the church is, perhaps, the fastest growing model in recent decades.[58] As noted above, theologians often combine this image with the kingly image to form a priest-king hybrid.[59] I already assessed this hybrid in connection with the Kingly Church. So, here I focus on the widespread depiction of priests as those who serve as mediators between God and humans. Such priests serve in a wide variety of ways. They lead in proper worship, offer divine blessings, and teach God's ways. The promise of this model resides in its biblical support at key places in the formation of God's people. It also gives necessary priority to the church's place in God's mission and emphasizes the

---

57. 1 John 2:2.

58. E.g., Beale, *The Temple and God's Mission*; Tom Greggs, *Dogmatic Ecclesiology*, vol. 1., *The Priestly Catholicity of the Church* (Grand Rapids, MI: Baker Academic, 2019); John Bergsma, *Jesus and the Old Testament Roots of the Priesthood* (Steubenville, OH: Emmaus Road Publishing, 2021); Nicholas Haydock, *The Theology of the Levitical Priesthood: Assisting God's People in Their Mission to the Nations* (Eugene, OR: Wipf & Stock, 2015); and Stefan Paas, *Pilgrims and Priests: Christian Mission in a Post-Christian Society* (London: SCM Press, 2019).

59. The Bible Project devotes an entire series of videos to this priest-king hybrid image: https://bibleproject.com/explore/category/the-royal-priest-series. See especially the video "Royal Priests of Eden." N. T. Wright develops this theme in *After You Believe*, building on the work of John Walton and G. K. Beale. Bergsma and Paas build on Beale's work insofar as they begin their account of the priestly vocation with Adam's responsibility in the garden of Eden. These scholars may be on to something when they see priestly parallels in the garden of Eden. However, Genesis associates this role with humanity in general and not with God's chosen people in particular. By way of contrast, Scripture spells out the priestly image in unambiguous terms at key points in the life of both Israel and the church.

holiness of God's people.[60] At its best the Priestly Church, like the Servant Church, acknowledges that God's people exist *for the world* as a part of God's plan to redeem the world.[61]

Though the Priestly Church enjoys extensive biblical and theological support, noteworthy weaknesses reduce its strength as a posture for relating to the world. To begin, priestly terminology carries considerable negative baggage, both in the Bible and throughout church history. Biblically speaking, Israel's priests broke faith with God's covenant with Israel. They were partly responsible for God's judgment on his people, which led to exile and the demise of Israelite political sovereignty. They had become so spiritually blind by the first century that they could not recognize Jesus as Messiah and handed him over to be executed by the Romans. Historically speaking, Christian priests in service to the church have also faltered. They are often remembered for compromising politically during the Holy Roman Empire, blessing bloodshed during the Crusades, and engaging in pedophilia with countless youth entrusted to their care. Of course, these moments capture priesthood at its worst. We must not presume that it accurately represents normal priestly service within Israel and the church. Still, it accounts for why many in our day might hesitate before associating priestly language with the church's witness to the world.

A more theological reservation about the priestly model gains traction from the high priesthood of Jesus. As the nation of Israel was crumbling at the hands of Babylon, Jeremiah prophesied of a coming day when God would make a new covenant with his people that would surpass the old one (Jer 31:1–24). The book of Hebrews argues quite decisively that Jesus not only instituted this new covenant but completely fulfilled the purpose and function of the old covenant and its priesthood.[62] That being the case, does it even make sense to reclaim the priestly image for

---

60. Priestly passages include Gen 12:2–3 (for blessing as a priestly function, cf. Num 6:23–27; Deut 10:8; and 21:5); Exod 19:5–6; Isa 61:1–9 (which Jesus appropriates to frame his mission in Luke 4:18–19); Rom 12:1–2; 15:15–16; 1 Pet 2:4–9; Rev 1:5–6; 5:9–10; and 20:6. Passages emphasizing the holiness of God's people include Lev 11:44–45; 19:2; 20:7, 26; 21:6–8; 2 Cor 6:14–18; 7:1; Eph 4:22–24; 1 Thess 4:4, 7; Heb 12:13–14; 1 Pet 1:14–16; and 2 Pet 3:11. Paul refers to Christians as saints or holy ones in multiple places (Rom 1:7; 1 Cor 1:2; 2 Cor 1:1; Eph 1:1; and Phil 1:1).

61. This makes it easy to combine the servant and priestly models into a hybrid model with different emphases, which is precisely what Paas does in *Pilgrims and Priests*, 175–177.

62. Heb 7–10.

the church? We are a new covenant people whose sole priest is the Lord, Jesus Christ. Far be it from us to appropriate language for ourselves that now belongs only to him.

Perhaps most problematic is the Priestly Church's tendency to define priestly service in terms of spiritual mediation between individuals and God. This bodes poorly for a generation that rightly rejects any form of religion that champions the vertical dimensions of faith independent of the horizontal dimensions.[63] Many churches have focused on the "spiritual" for so long that we may even be experiencing an overcorrection that elevates the social and political aspects of faith to the neglect of moral and spiritual transformation in the lives of individuals. People today may perceive a witnessing model that focuses on what the church uniquely has to offer this world as an untimely reversion to a problematic dichotomy between the spiritual and social, the vertical and horizontal.

A final limitation, similar to one of the Prophetic Church, is that Israel's priests performed their priestly service on behalf of fellow Israelites with whom they shared a common covenant.[64] Since we are considering how the church ought to relate to the unbelieving world, it goes without saying that the world has not agreed to the new covenant that God has initiated through Christ. To the extent that they have not asked for our priestly service, we would be forcing our beliefs upon others against the free will that God gave them to reject the offer of salvation. This same limitation does not apply to unbelievers who freely look to the church for spiritual direction, as in the case of Roman soldiers asking John the Baptist what they must do.

Given these liabilities, one might find the Priestly Church hardly worth exploring. Indeed, none of the models surveyed thus far fares particularly well. Yet I stand by this typology because it aligns quite well with the major approaches to church-world relations in our day. I also believe that the priestly model possesses great untapped potential when conceived more holistically. The rest of this book taps into that potential.

---

63. John Stott captures these sentiments well in *Issues Facing Christianity Today: New Perspectives on Social and Moral Dilemmas.* (Basingstoke, UK: Marshall Pickering, 1984), 24.

64. Cf. Exod 24:1–8 and Deut 26:16–19.

CHAPTER TWO

Priestly Renewal

> To him who loves us and freed us from our sins by his blood, and made us
> to be a kingdom, priests serving his God and Father, to him be glory and
> dominion forever and ever.
>
> (Rev 1:5–6)

PRIESTLY MODEL REVISED

Priestly status is the first blessing God confers on the Israelites when he claims them as his people in Exodus, and it is one of the last images he leaves us with in Revelation. As a model for capturing the nature of church-world relations it has a lot going for it. It enjoys strong biblical support, it prioritizes what God's people uniquely have to offer, and it emphasizes the set-apart nature of the church.

Still the priestly model, as typically conceived, possesses significant liabilities. Israel and the church's priests left much to be desired legacy-wise. Priesthood language tends to emphasize vertical more than horizontal relationships and elevates the "spiritual" at the expense of the social. Furthermore, according to Hebrews, the new covenant in Jesus fulfilled and brought to a decisive end the old covenant's reliance upon sacred sanctuaries, sacrificial systems, and a sanctified priestly class. Finally, since believers don't share a common covenant with unbelievers, as Israel's priests did with fellow Israelites, we should be careful how we apply priestly particulars to Christian witness.

A MORE HOLISTIC APPROACH

For the priesthood to shed helpful light on how the church should relate to the world, the above liabilities must be addressed. Fortunately, Scripture addresses each one when we take into consideration *all* Levites and not just the Aaronic priests who served in the sanctuary. This is seldom done. The sons of Aaron were most famous for offering sacrifices that atoned for sin and made ongoing divine–human communion possible. But that only represents one aspect of Israel's priestly heritage, significant as that aspect may be.

Many Christians think of priestly responsibility in Aaronic terms because their priestly frame of reference is limited mostly to the New Testament book of Hebrews. The priestly material in Torah can be difficult to comprehend. So people often consult Hebrews 4–10 as if it were a sort of Cliff's Notes summary of the Old Testament priesthood. The Aaronic priesthood features prominently in Hebrews because this sermonic letter argues that Jesus's blood atones for human sin once and for all, thereby fulfilling the ultimate purpose of the sacrificial system. This focus leads Christians to limit priestly responsibility to our vertical or spiritual relationship with God to the neglect of horizontal or social witness.

This approach hardly does justice to the full biblical teaching. For starters, sin sacrifices were not the only sacrifices. Many offerings were celebratory in nature and involved feasting with loved ones and neighbors as well as providing for the poor.[1] Also, many of the sin offerings required acts of restitution that set right certain social wrongs.[2] Israel's sacrificial system contained important horizontal dimensions that are routinely ignored. Moreover, Aaron's sons were not the only priests in Israel, and the majority of priests never presided over the sacrificial system. These other priests, often referred to simply as Levites, tended to the setup, teardown, and relocation of the tabernacle. They also fulfilled a variety of priestly responsibilities remotely in the various towns in which they lived, scattered throughout each of Israel's twelve territories. Representative responsibilities included distancing themselves from tribal governance, overseeing cities of refuge, safeguarding the sanctity of life, studying and teaching God's word, and

---

1. E.g., sacrifices of well-being (Lev 3:1–17) and celebratory offerings, including Passover and the Festival of Weeks (Deut 16:1–12).

2. E.g., Num 5:5–8.

leading God's people in truthful praise. These lesser-known priestly duties played a vital role in the spiritual *and* social well-being of all Israelites. God's mission to the world through Israel depended on them. They therefore furnish a fuller understanding of Israelite priesthood that offsets key limitations of the Aaronic priestly model for capturing the church's relationship to the world.

OVERCOMING PRIESTLY LIMITATIONS

With a more holistic view of priesthood in mind, we may now revisit the aforementioned shortcomings of the priestly model. Consider first the tainted legacy of biblical and postbiblical priests. Within the Old Testament itself, Israel's priests neglected and perverted their priestly responsibilities, and God eventually stripped them of those responsibilities. This could have been the end, but it wasn't. Jesus redeemed Israel's fallen priesthood by succeeding where they failed. In so doing, he fulfilled the priesthood of Israel and empowered his followers to share in key aspects of *his* continued priestly service to the world. I develop this theme at length in chapter 6.

At this point, I need to make a fundamental observation. It speaks to *how* Jesus fulfilled Israel's priesthood. In identifying with our humanity, sharing in our suffering, and triumphing over our sin, Jesus became the perfect high priest. He therefore redeemed the image of priesthood for God's people. But this does not mean that the church should appoint new priests to serve within the church in a manner akin to Israel's priests.[3] The New Testament church steers clear of all such appointments. Rather the apostolic witness testifies that Christ forgave the sins of the entire Israelite nation and, in so doing, restored its collective calling to be a kingdom of priests that blesses all nations. The failure of Israel's priests did not disqualify the Israelites from their vital place in God's mission. Jesus, the ultimate high priest, has placed the derailed train of salvation history back on its tracks. For this reason, New Testament apostles as prominent as Peter, Paul, and John felt quite comfortable applying priestly language to the church as a whole, and so should we.[4]

Those who object most strongly to the priestly model for church-world relations fear that it might steer the church back into the rut of reducing Christian

---

3. Jesus also redeemed Israel's kingship by coming as the Messiah. However, he did not restore any sort of kingship for or among his people prior to the eschaton (cf. Rev 2:26; 5:10; and 22:5).

4. E.g., Rom 12:1–2; 1 Pet 2:4–5; and Rev 1:5–6.

witness to the vertical task of getting people right with God. Broadening our notion of priesthood to include the entire priestly tribe of Levi helps immensely in this regard. Israel's scattered Levitical priests foreground the horizontal dimensions of priestly service without leaving behind the necessary vertical dimensions. Indeed, they show us that the vertical and horizontal must not be separated at all. We do not truly have one without the other, for they are intricately interwoven.

Expanding the scope of priestly service in this way reckons with the undeniable fact that Israel's priests served fellow Israelites bound to a common covenant, whereas the church relates to a world that does not share a common covenant. How can we serve the world in priestly fashion when, for all intents and purposes, we occupy completely different worlds? How do we avoid the Prophetic Church's error of holding people accountable for commitments they never made?

I address these questions at length in chapter 4, but I'll provide a brief explanation here. The wider population of Levites inherited no tribal territory of their own. God scattered them among all of Israel's tribes where they resided like aliens and exiles. Their exilic status wasn't just about property deeds; it meant that all Levites remained outsiders to tribal governance and politics. They could not serve as elders, officials, or even soldiers among their host tribes. They were freed from such community service so they could focus on priestly matters that only they were equipped to handle.

So even though all Israelites shared a common covenant that linked their lives in important ways, their priests remained outsiders who didn't quite fit in because they had different priorities and responsibilities. The Levites bore additional covenant responsibilities—a priestly covenant within a covenant—which held them to higher standards than ordinary citizens in their host tribes. This outsider status, with its increased expectations, parallels the church's relationship to the world in key ways that make the priestly model particularly insightful and timely.

THE APPROACH AND SCOPE OF THIS BOOK

Scholars have added significantly to our understanding of Israel's priests in recent years. A good number of them shed valuable light on the historical complexity of Israelite priesthood and its functional evolution well into the

New Testament period. They've done some fascinating work in reconstructing the historical origins of Israel's priests in light of biblical texts and ancient Near Eastern analogues.[5] Other scholars focus more on the contemporary relevance of Israel's priests, whether to Roman Catholic polity, biblical theology, or Christian mission.[6]

In this book, I focus most on socially significant aspects of Israelite priesthood that find New Testament backing in one way or another. By New Testament backing I mean that the apostolic writings call believers to a posture or function typical of Old Testament priests. I strive to avoid assigning priestly functions to the church that the New Testament itself does not assign. The twin foci of social significance and New Testament backing shed valuable light on the church's priestly relationship to the world.

I also focus on how the Bible presents the priesthood in the final form of Scripture as we have it. I recognize that the history behind the text proves far more complicated than the bits and pieces we find in Scripture. The final authors and editors were certainly aware of this. Their portraits contain more than just historical records. Like all good narrators, they crafted and shaped their priestly accounts to convey the values and priorities most important

---

5. E.g., Deborah W. Rooke, *Zadok's Heirs: The Role and Development of the High Priesthood in Ancient Israel* (Oxford: Oxford University Press, 2000); Aelred Cody, *A History of the Old Testament Priesthood*, Analecta Biblica 35 (Rome: Pontifical Biblical Institute, 1969); James C. VanderKam, *From Joshua to Caiaphas: High Priests after the Exile* (Minneapolis: Fortress Press, 2004); Joseph Blenkinsopp, *Sage, Prophet, Priest: Religious and Intellectual Leadership in Ancient Israel* (Louisville, KY: John Knox Press, 1995); Richard D. Nelson, *Raising Up a Faithful Priest: Community and Priesthood in Biblical Theology* (Louisville, KY: Westminster/John Knox Press, 1993); Martha Himmelfarb, *A Kingdom of Priests: Ancestry and Merit in Ancient Judaism* (Philadelphia: University of Pennsylvania, 2006).

6. Pass, *Pilgrims and Priests*. Pass does a masterful job unpacking the post-Christendom nature of Western Christianity, highlighting the church's pilgrim status. He then uses the priestly image to frame certain aspects of Christian mission. Yet he never quite acknowledges the extent to which priests were themselves pilgrims among the other tribes of Israel. He writes as if the church's pilgrim nature is an accident of history that we must reckon with and not a key part of priestly identity itself in Scripture. In *Theology of the Levitical Priesthood*, Haydock keenly addresses the landless nature of the priests (55–63). Their landlessness makes up part of his wider theology of priesthood, which includes several other key dimensions. Though he affirms the relevance of Israel's priests for the church, he doesn't get into specifics much. He writes mostly about the biblical themes themselves. For the remainder of this book, I connect what Pass keeps separate—priests and pilgrims—and develop the church's priestly vocation in much greater detail than Haydock.

to them and the communities they served. Since we are concerned with the priesthood's meaning for God's people going forward, their cumulative narrative portrait ideally serves our purposes.

With this approach, I identify five aspects of the priestly calling that enrich our understanding of the church's relationship to the world: residence, hospitality, stewardship, witness, and praise.

- Residence: Scattered throughout all of Israel's tribes, the Levites trusted God alone as their portion and remained relatively detached from the places they lived and cultures they inhabited.
- Hospitality: Tasked with extending hospitality rather than lethal judgment to Israel's most wanted public offenders, God excused the Levites from policing their host lands and empowered them to mediate God's peace to all the land's inhabitants.
- Stewardship: As stewards of sacrifice, the Levites upheld God's exclusive claim on all life—not just in the tabernacle, but in their dining rooms and on the battlefield.
- Witness: As experts in Torah, the Levites preserved the divinely ordained way of life that promotes flourishing for all creation and forms Israel into a powerful witness to all nations.
- Praise: When reduced to court musicians by Israel's kings, the Levites found creative ways to maintain their critical voice and sing powerfully and peacefully before all people and authorities.

This fivefold priestly portrait sheds valuable light on the church's relationship to the world. It doesn't include all the priestly attributes that God's people might embody, but it greatly enriches the priestly model of the church. To abandon this priestly calling or to compromise any of its key components amounts to making a fundamental shift in the strategic way God has deployed his chosen people for the sake of this world.

In chapters 4–8, I discuss each component of the priestly posture in three ways. First, I reach back into Scripture to discuss a formative event in the life or legacy of Israel's priests. I then demonstrate how this event set a trajectory both for the wider people of Israel and the Christian church. Second, I briefly discuss what this means for the big picture of how God has called the church to relate to himself and to the world. Third, I unpack several implications of this posture for the church's life together and its witness to unbelievers.

Before considering these five attributes in depth, in chapter 3 I locate Israel's priests within the story of Israel as a whole. That story itself is located in the story of God's redeeming love for a world enslaved to sin.

PRIESTLY CAVEAT

Though the priestly image has been around for a long time, it hasn't really caught on as a governing metaphor for the church, especially in its relationship to unbelievers. I suspect this relates at least partly to how the priestly image has been used. As previously mentioned, teachers often present priests as spiritual mediators between people and God, since Israel's priests are typically associated with offering sin sacrifices to God. Christ fulfilled this function without remainder. That being the case, Christ followers are often reluctant to see themselves serving in a similar way.

Such reticence is reinforced by the fact that throughout church history the priestly title has been used primarily of clergy. High church circles especially perpetuate this image—mostly with reference to their role in presiding over the Eucharist. The priesthood thus sounds way too Roman Catholic for many Protestants and just plain outdated to those seeking to purge the church of all archaic-sounding jargon. In sum, people think of the priestly role as spiritual in function and limited to an elite class of old-school Christians.

Yet for several decades Christians have sought to recover the sorely overlooked social and political dimensions of the church's nature and mission. Many churches focused on what they could offer unbelievers spiritually, to the neglect of the gospel's meaning socially.[7] Thus, more political and social images—like prophet, king, and servant—have understandably taken center stage. They seem more relevant to the needed corrective. In this context, the thought of emphasizing the church's priestly dimensions may seem like

---

7. In *Scandalous Witness: A Little Political Manifesto for Christians* (Grand Rapids, MI: Eerdmans, 2020), Lee C. Camp frames this temptation in terms of chaplaincy: "as chaplain, Christianity reduces itself to mere spirituality, to some form of inner peace that has little to do with social or political realities; thus the most violent or unjust of deeds can be blessed with some bit of holiness, some prayer, some holy oil or sacrament" (46).

reverting to an emphasis on spiritual rites detached from the church's social and political mandate.[8]

Let me be clear: I am *not* suggesting that in this book. On the contrary, I am convinced that the priestly image best captures the church's social and political witness without neglecting spiritual matters. Unfortunately, because people have primarily framed priestly duties in spiritualistic terms, they have largely overlooked the priests' social and political contributions.[9] The priestly framework I provide in chapters 4–8 foregrounds these neglected contributions. To fully appreciate them, we must first locate them within the story of God's people as a whole.

---

8. Such sentiments would echo nineteenth- to twentieth-century higher critical approaches to the history of religion in which scholars disparaged priests for being rigid institutionalists as opposed to viewing them as more dynamic and spirit-filled. Cf. Blenkinsopp, *Sage, Prophet, Priest*, 66–68, and Nelson, *Raising up a Faithful Priest*, 101–105.

9. It probably doesn't help that the politically-minded priests we encounter in the New Testament conspired with Roman authorities to kill Jesus.

CHAPTER THREE

Kingdom and Kin

Israel was not the first or only nation to have priests. Long before Moses ordained Levi's sons, Abraham paid tithes to a mysterious Palestinian priest name Melchizedek. Joseph and Moses married the daughters of foreign priests. And Pharaoh gave special privileges to the priests of Egypt.[1] Ancient Philistines, Canaanites, and Babylonians also employed priests, as do members of contemporary religions like Buddhism, Hinduism, and Shinto.[2]

One could map out the functions of these diverse religious functionaries and identify some common ground, but that would hardly do justice to any of them. Many popular misconceptions about Israel's priests are rooted in vague notions of what all priests tend to do, namely, mediate between the human and the divine. If we want to gain a firm grasp on Israelite priesthood, we need to locate it within the specific story of God and his people.

In this chapter, I provide the backstory to Israel's priests in terms of seven stages from Genesis to Exodus 19. This is not so much the Levite's story in particular, which I get to in future chapters, but the birth of the priestly kingdom of Israel as a whole. We cannot understand the tribe of Levi apart from their wider Israelite kin. After telling this story, I highlight a few key principles about how the Levites related to fellow, less-priestly citizens of God's priestly kingdom.

---

1. See Gen 14:18; 41:45; 47:22; and Exod 3:1.
2. See 1 Sam 5:5; 2 Kgs 10:19; and Bel and the Dragon 1:8–21 (part of the Greek additions to Daniel, which are included in the Apocrypha).

BIRTH OF A PRIESTLY KINGDOM

Just as we misunderstand Israel's priests apart from their place in Israel's story, so we misunderstand Israel itself apart from the story of God's effort to rescue the whole world. The entire Bible tells the story of this rescue. We can summarize it in terms of five scenes: Creation's Collapse (Gen 1–11), Called Community (Gen 12—Mal), Christ (Matt—John), Commissioned Community (Acts—Jude), and Creation's Consummation (Rev).

We are concerned here with the beginning of that story, the first two scenes. It provides the necessary background for the priestly calling of Israel as a whole and Levi's descendants in particular. The covenant code of Torah—Exodus 20 through Deuteronomy—spells out the calling and responsibilities of Israel's priests. Genesis 1 through Exodus 19 recounts their basic backstory. From creation to covenant, these chapters show how God began forming Abraham's descendants—eventually called Israel—into a priestly kingdom that exists first and foremost for the sake of this world. I survey these events in terms of seven episodes.

1. Creation

The Bible begins with two creation accounts, one of which nests within the other like a Russian matryoshka doll. Genesis 1 opens with a panoramic view of all creation framed in terms of six days. Over the first three days, God forms several distinct domains: day and night, sky and sea, and land. Over the next three days God fills those domains with their appointed occupants: celestial bodies, birds and fish, animals and humans. All was good, each step of the way. God declared it "very good" after he crowned creation with humanity (v. 31).

Genesis 2 begins by highlighting God's rest on day seven. It then transitions to a second creation account that focuses on days 3 and 6, God's work with the land, animals, and humans. Everything seemed fine again, until God pointed out the first not-so-good thing: "It is *not good* for the man to be alone" (v. 18). God quickly remedies this deficiency by creating woman out of man, much like he created man from the soil. All of creation was interdependent, and that was a good thing! By chapter end, the man and woman were at peace with one another and presumably also with God and nonhuman creation.

2. Collapse

In both accounts, God places creation in the care of humans. In the second account, God places limits on human responsibility. The forbidden fruit in the midst of the garden stood as a perpetual reminder that this world belongs to God and not humans. We serve as stewards of his treasures and may not do with them whatever we wish. We are caretakers, not kings. In Genesis 3, we learn that the humans didn't take kindly to such limitations on their power and status. Tragically, they conspire with the wisest garden creature in an effort to transcend their limitations and become more like God.

Their conspiracy results in a whole new world, but not the kind they hoped for. In Genesis 3:14–19, God declares the sorry state of affairs that results from this pitiable power grab. The humans grow estranged from God, one another, and nonhuman creation. Furthermore, both human and nonhuman creation subject themselves to decay, degeneration, and ultimately death. Theologians refer to this catastrophic turn of events as *the fall*. All that was good in creation has fallen from perfect harmony to perpetual turmoil—from life giving to death dealing. There was no going back. God drove the humans from the garden so they could not eat the forever fruit of the tree of life. They must now face the harsh and unyielding reality they created for themselves.

3. Commitment

Things unfold just like God declared. Exploitation and violence erupt throughout the earth. It begins with the first family in chapter 4, continues through their descendants, and expands to a global pandemic by Genesis 6. The creator grieves over his creation because he knows what must be done. Before humans can destroy the world altogether, God floods the earth of all wickedness and preserves enough of each species for a fresh start.

For this new start to be genuinely good, it couldn't take place under constant threat of another global purge. So God appoints the rainbow to remind humans of his commitment to all creation, never to destroy it again. This commitment sets the stage for salvation history. In promising never to flood the earth, God places the burden on himself to find some way to save this world from a human race bent on distorting and destroying everything good. Having removed the threat of annihilation, God must pioneer a new initiative to ensure that his will is done on earth as in heaven.

4. Calling

God's new initiative begins with Genesis 12:1–3. God chooses Abraham and makes a fourfold promise to him. Abraham's descendants would become a numerous *people*. God would lead them to a specific *place*. They would enjoy a *privileged* relationship with God. They would carry out God's *purpose* of being a blessing to all nations. The realization of this promise drives the narrative of Torah and Israel's history going forward. According to the apostle Peter, the early church inherits this same promise through Jesus: "You are the descendants of the prophets and of the covenant that God gave to your ancestors, saying to Abraham, 'And in your descendants all the families of the earth shall be blessed' " (Acts 3:25).

Abraham's descendants stood at the center of God's strategy for overcoming the fallen world's problems spelled out in Genesis 1–11. Through them, God fulfilled his promise never to flood the world again. They were God's pioneering initiative. For God so loved the world, he called Abraham's descendants to bless the world. God's chosen people were not a provincial religion that God started in order to give the people of Palestine something to live for. God's people existed for the whole world's sake. They were set apart, like priests, to impart God's blessing—not just to Abraham and his immediate sons, but to the entire lot of his descendants.

5. Cultivation

The rest of Genesis tells the story of Abraham and his offspring's privileged relationship with God. God guides them to the land that he promised Abraham and protects them through adversity from within and without. Multiple times, he delivers them from kings, armies, famines, and even barren wombs. They survive and, in fact, thrive by divine miracle alone. God was keeping his promise and would never abandon his purpose.

God sustained his promise even when famine forced God's people to relocate to Egypt. Abraham and Sarah had given birth to Isaac. Isaac and Rebekah had given birth to Jacob, who was called Israel. Jacob and his wives had given birth to twelve sons—the twelve sons of Israel—one of whom was Levi, the namesake of Israel's priesthood. These sons and their families grew to seventy in number before the famine of famines struck the western fertile crescent. All of Palestine, and even Egypt, would be affected. Through divine providence, the Israelites migrated to northern Egypt where they could feed their children, sustain their livelihood, and multiply exponentially. They did so without being absorbed into the wider population because the Egyptians would not eat, let alone mate, with lowly shepherds.

6. Captivity

Pharaoh felt threatened by the Israelites' prosperity. So much so, Exodus 1 tells us, that he made slaves of God's people and subjected them to forced labor. Yet that could not stop God's blessing, and the Israelites continued to multiply. Though Pharaoh intensified their labor beyond reason and slew their newborns in rage, with anguished cries they continued to multiply. And God heard their cry. Remembering his promise, "the one who curses you I will curse" (Gen 12:3), God turned his attention to Pharaoh.

Through the staff of Moses, God unleashed upon Egypt plague after horrific plague (Exod 7–12). Eventually, Pharaoh relented and Moses led the Israelites out of Egypt, through the Red Sea, and into the Sinai Peninsula. Providing food from heaven and fending off foes, God blessed his chosen people so they might someday bless the world.

7. Covenant

Upon finally reaching Mount Sinai, the Israelites set up camp and God met with Moses to reveal his will for them. At this time, through Moses, God formally introduced himself to the Israelites, saying, "You have seen what I did to the Egyptians, and how I bore you on eagles' wings and brought you to myself. Now therefore, if you obey my voice and keep my covenant, you shall be my treasured possession out of all the peoples. Indeed, the whole earth is mine, but you shall be for me a priestly kingdom and a holy nation" (Exod 19:4–6). God had anointed the Israelites multiple times, with spattered doorposts, Red Sea torrents, and heavenly manna. But here, for the first time, he claims them as his priests.

The phrase "priestly kingdom" clearly parallels "holy nation." They are two ways of saying the same thing. "Priestly" and "holy" point to Israel's set-apart status. "Kingdom" and "nation" speak to their collective identity. God sets Israel apart as a nation, from the nations, for the nations. Holy objects always serve a special purpose. They are distinguished from common objects not because of their inherent superiority but because they serve an uncommon purpose. Exodus 19 does not spell out Israel's purpose, but the covenant God makes with them presumes the Abrahamic calling to be a blessing to all nations. This episode continues the story of creation's collapse recounted in Genesis 1–11. God's covenant people play the central role in God's strategy for restoring fallen creation and reconciling broken relationships.

PRIESTLY PRINCIPLES

Beginning in Exodus 20, God reveals his will for his people. He makes a bilateral covenant that stipulates both how all Israelites should live their lives and how God will bless them if they do. This blessed way of life remained central to how God wills to use his people as a blessing to all nations. Moses introduces the covenant this way to the second generation of Israelites who were about to enter the Promised Land:

> See, just as the LORD my God has charged me, I now teach you statutes
> and ordinances for you to observe in the land that you are about to
> enter and occupy. You must observe them diligently, for this will show
> your wisdom and discernment to the peoples, who, when they hear all
> these statutes, will say, "Surely this great nation is a wise and discerning
> people!" For what other great nation has a god so near to it as the LORD
> our God is whenever we call to him? (Deut 4:5–7)

Should the Israelites keep God's commands, to use Isaiah's language, they will shine like a light to the nations.[3] Within this covenant with his priestly people, God sets apart Levi's descendants to serve him as priests—a sort of priesthood within a priesthood.[4] Their sacred food, attire, and connection to Israel's farming and childbearing practices convey key priestly principles. These principles unite the five priestly attributes showcased in this book and help solidify the priestly posture as a compelling model for church-world relations.

---

3. Isa 42:6; 49:6; 51:4; and 60:3.

4. Exodus 32 tells the story of how the Levites became priests. I discuss this story at length in ch. 6. The Levites were not the first to serve as priests among the Israelites. They apparently had functioning priests even before agreeing to the covenant with God (Exod 19:24). Aaron's sons were also granted priestly responsibilities in Exodus 28, though they, too, were Levites (Exod 4:14).

Food and Clothing

Israel's priests performed a wide variety of functions. One of the most sacred functions, carried out by only a select few, entailed serving in the holy place of the tabernacle. All Israelites could enter the tabernacle's outer courtyard to bring their offerings. But only certain priests, Aaron's sons, could enter the holy place. There they burned incense each morning and evening. There they also ate the bread of presence—*twelve* loaves total, representing the twelve tribes of Israel. The priests placed this bread on the table of presence and had to replenish it each sabbath. This sacred food reminded them that God set them apart *from* the other tribes *for* the other tribes.

A lampstand provided light for the holy place. Israelite artisans made everything inside the holy place of gold: the altar of incense, the table of showbread, and the lampstand. By way of contrast, they furnished the outer courtyard in bronze. The most holy place, the holy of holies, also contained gold furnishing, namely the ark of the covenant. Only the high priest entered the most holy place and they did so only once a year, on the Day of Atonement.

Entering these holy spaces was such a sacred duty that Aaron's sons had to don specific vestments before doing so. These vestments were also sacred.[5] Spirit-led craftsmen created the originals from voluntary spirit-led donations by the Israelites.[6] Key components of the breastplate, ephod, and turban reminded Israel's priests of their unique calling. The turban contained a pure gold rosette engraved with the words "Holy to the Lord." Four rows of three stones adorned the breast piece. Each stone corresponded to one of the twelve tribes of Israel. On the shoulders of the ephod hung two onyx stones. An inscriber etched the names of six of Jacob's sons into each one, twelve total, once again representing Israel's twelve tribes.

This priestly attire spoke powerfully to those who wore it and to anyone who looked upon it. It conveyed two clear commitments: sanctity and solidarity. God set them apart *from* the people (sanctity) and *for* the people (solidarity). To be a priest meant being part of the few who existed on behalf of the many.

The same holds true for Israel and the church as a whole. God separated Israel as a priestly nation so they might exist for the sake of all nations. Christ

---

5. Exod 28:1–43 offers the most detailed account of these vestments.
6. Exod 35:21.

renewed this identity for the church. We exist as a kingdom of priests who stand *apart* from the world and *for* the world (1 Pet 2:9).

Farming and Childbearing

Numbers 3 conveys similar sentiments. Farmers deemed the first of their crops and flocks as sacred. They were the best because they signified fruitful fields and wombs, and thus a secure future. For this reason, the Israelites offered their first fruits to God in worship. This entailed traveling to the place of God's presence, feasting before the Lord with one's family, and sharing with the Lord's priests.[7]

Likewise, children born in their parents' youth represented the strength and vitality of their parents.[8] When God separated the Israelites from Egypt at the expense of Egypt's firstborn sons, he claimed every firstborn Israelite son as his own.[9] Though he regarded the whole nation as his firstborn son,[10] in a special way each firstborn male would represent his family before the Lord, presumably in a priestly capacity. God later claimed the entire tribe of Levi to stand in for all of Israel's firstborn sons.[11] The Levites, then, came to represent the first fruits of the wombs of all Israelite families. They represented the best of God's provision and thus a secure future. Israel's priests held together Israel's rich past and hopeful future. In a real sense, they *embodied* the future of Israel.

James says something remarkably similar about the church: "In fulfillment of his own purpose he gave us birth by the word of truth, so that we would become a kind of first fruits of his creatures" (Jas 1:18). God sovereignly purposed to redeem and restore all of creation. This defines the future of world history, and God accepts the kingdom community, the church, as the first fruits of this glorious reality. Like Israel's holy priests, who existed on behalf of all Israel, God's holy church exists on behalf of all creation—all people, all critters, all throughout the earth.

---

7. Deut 15:19–20 and 18:4.
8. Gen 49:3.
9. Exod 13:2, 11–16.
10. Exod 4:22.
11. Num 3:12–51.

CHAPTER FOUR

In-Residence

PRIESTLY LEGACY

Levi was the great ancestor of Israel's priesthood. He was the third son of Jacob through his wife Leah. All we know about Levi's life consists of one act of violence, recorded in Genesis 34.

After two decades serving his uncle Laban, Levi's father Jacob took his wives and kids and headed south toward the Promised Land of Canaan. After successfully negotiating his way out of perilous encounters—with Laban, then an angel of the Lord, and finally his brother Esau—Jacob faced a fourth trial on his way home. Shortly after settling in northern Canaan, Shechem, a prince of that region, raped Jacob's daughter, Dinah. The prince's father, Hamor, sought to appease Jacob by proposing that Dinah marry his impulsive son. This marriage would join these families in a peaceful alliance and somewhat restore Dinah's dignity. Jacob agreed under one condition: all the men of Hamor's tribe must be circumcised, just like Jacob and his sons. Hamor accepted this condition and Jacob's woes appeared to be over. He had made a powerful military ally, secured a reliable trading partner, found a way to marry off his children without returning to conniving Laban, and could finally settle down in his own land in peace.

Levi and Simeon had other plans. Dinah was their full sister, also born to Leah. Her rape was personal to them. Shechem dishonored her and her brothers, and their father's solution was unacceptable. So, while all the men of Hamor were recovering from this minor but temporarily debilitating surgery, Levi and Simeon made their way through the camp, slaughtered every male, and seized their possessions like spoils of war. Jacob was livid. He rebuked them, saying, "You have brought trouble on me by making me odious to the inhabitants of the land, the Canaanites and the Perizzites; my numbers are few, and if they gather themselves against me and attack me, I shall be destroyed, both I and my household" (Gen 34:30).

Simeon and Levi justified their actions: "Should our sister be treated like a whore?" (v. 31). Though Jacob's fears were never realized, he never forgot the risk he incurred on account of these vengeful sons. On his deathbed, he pronounced a curse upon them and their offspring, saying, "Simeon and Levi are brothers; weapons of violence are their swords. May I never come into their council; may I not be joined to their company—for in their anger they killed men, and at their whim they hamstrung oxen. Cursed be their anger, for it is fierce, and their wrath, for it is cruel! *I will divide them in Jacob, and scatter them in Israel*" (Gen 49:5–7).

Their fateful scattering took effect several centuries later, after the Israelites fled Egypt and settled into the land of Canaan. For Simeon, it meant receiving only a small plot of land within the territory of Judah, the most prominent southern tribe.[1] For Levi and his priestly descendants, it meant being dispersed throughout all of Israel's tribes. They had to live forever as aliens and exiles in the territory of others.

Their exilic status is first codified in Numbers 18:20, where the Lord tells Levi's descendant Aaron, "You shall have no allotment in their land, nor shall you have any share among them." God had appointed Aaron's sons to be a special class of Levites with unique responsibilities. Yet they were not the only Levites to be scattered throughout the land. All of Jacob's sons received large swaths of land in Canaan, except for the Levites.[2] Instead, God required the other tribes to carve out space within their territories so each male Levite could settle down and raise his family. The Levites received 48 towns all together: 13 within the territory of Judah, Simeon, and Benjamin; 10 within Ephraim, Dan, and the western portion of Manasseh; 13 within Issachar, Asher, Naphtali, and the eastern portion of Manasseh; and 12 within Reuben, Gad, and Zebulun.[3] These towns were theirs to manage and could not be taken from them,[4] but other tribes owned and ruled the territory within which they were located.

---

1. See Josh 19:9.
2. See Deut 18:1–2; Num 35:1–5; Josh 14:1–3; 18:7; and 21:1–41.
3. Josh 21.
4. Lev 25:32–34.

Since Levites could never become landowners, they could never become independently wealthy. Wherever they lived, they remained resident aliens. In the laws of Torah, they were frequently grouped among the poor, powerless, and landless folk of Canaan. For instance, when other Israelites traveled to the tabernacle to give offerings and celebrate festivals, they were required to bring and provide for their children, their slaves, any strangers in their land, and whatever Levites settled among them.[5] Likewise, every three years, landowning tribes collected a special tithe so that resident aliens, orphans, widows, and Levites could come and eat their fill.[6] Israel's priestly people had to humble themselves and accept charity from their host tribes. They were numbered among the least of the land's inhabitants, with little room for upward social mobility. Each holiday pilgrimage reminded them of their lowly position.[7]

Yet God took Levi's curse and transformed it into a blessing. What Jacob meant as punishment, God turned into reward. I recount the fascinating story of how this happened in chapter 10, but for now it is important to note that, without revoking their lowly, landless status, God gave the Levites something better: the priesthood. Moses explains, "The levitical priests, the whole tribe of Levi, shall have no allotment or inheritance within Israel. *They may eat the sacrifices that are the LORD's portion* but they shall have no inheritance among the other members of the community; *the LORD is their inheritance*, as he promised them" (Deut 18:1–2). Inheriting the Lord didn't mean that only the Levites were God's chosen heirs; it meant that they were set apart to serve God and fellow Israelites in unique ways. That's what being a priest was all about. Some Levites served by offering sacred food; others took care of the tabernacle, taught Torah, managed cities of refuge, judged difficult cases, and discerned the Lord's will in matters of national urgency. The Levites carried out these functions not *despite* their lowly landless status but precisely *because* of it. Their exilic posture empowered them to perform these sensitive duties in an impartial manner. Their dispersion throughout the tribes made them a unique asset to God in carrying out his ultimate purposes for Israel and the world.

This was not the first time God scattered people for their own good. In Genesis 11, he dispersed the builders of Babel before they could effectively

---

5. Deut 12:12, 18–19; and 16:11–14.

6. Deut 14:28–29.

7. This reminds one of Jesus's instruction to his followers that they must become like children and slaves.

engineer their own demise. Humanity came together and sought to make a name for themselves by constructing an impressive city with a tower reaching into the heavens. God knew that such hubris, all too common among world empires like Babylon, would only lead to a small class of powerful people lording over the masses.[8] So, he confused their speech, which disrupted their communication, diluted their combined power, and ultimately led them to disperse throughout the world. This was God's plan from the beginning.[9] Though this scattering stood as judgment upon their pride, it also represented divine grace insofar as human thriving and dominion over creation required them to fill the earth and establish a diverse cultural tapestry that unfolds all of humanity's wonderful creative potential.

In the sixth century, God likewise scattered the nation of Israel throughout the ancient world. Despite Torah's design for their life together—as a loose federation of independent tribes—they built their own Babel-like empire with a glamorous centralized city, powerful worldly king, and weaponized standing army. Such structures routinely led to the oppression and enslavement of the masses.[10] As predicted in 1 Samuel 8, the Israelites had engineered their own demise. In response, God raised up—ironically—Babylon to raze their project to the ground and scatter them among the nations as exiles. To maintain some semblance of their identity as God's people, the Jews formed synagogues wherever they were scattered. This enabled them to order their lives according to Torah the best they could, which prepared them to answer God's call when he returned to restore his people and inaugurate his kingdom. This dispersion, too, was a blessing. In retrospect, we see that God's ultimate plan involved sending his chosen people throughout the world to make disciples of all nations. The earliest Christian missionaries, including Paul and Silas, made extensive use of exilic synagogues as strategic missionary posts. In each city, they first proclaimed the gospel in Jewish synagogues.[11] The resulting Jewish converts provided a stable nucleus for fledgling churches, which could then reach out to Gentiles. In this way, the gospel of Jesus spread rapidly and numerous churches were planted.

---

8. This story serves as a poignant critique of empires like Egypt, Assyria, Persia, and of course Babylon, after which Babel was likely named. Cf. Nugent, *Genesis 1–11*, 168–178.

9. Gen 1:22; 9:1, 7.

10. See John C. Nugent, *The Politics of Yahweh: John Howard Yoder, the Old Testament, and the People of God* (Eugene, OR: Cascade Books, 2011), ch. 4.

11. Acts 9:20; 13:5, 14; 14:1; 17:10; 18:4, 19, 26; and 19:8.

This pattern of providential scattering repeated with the earliest Christians. After receiving the Holy Spirit, the early church in Acts hesitated before going forth and proclaiming the gospel to all nations. They chose, instead, to congregate in and around Jerusalem. Then, in Acts 8:1, we read that a great persecution struck Jerusalem. All except the core apostles scattered, and so began the gospel's advance. The early church did not immediately view this persecution as a blessing, but God used it to launch his global mission. This is why the book of James is addressed to "the twelve tribes in the Dispersion" and the letter of 1 Peter to "the exiles of the Dispersion."[12] Exile often feels like a curse and sometimes truly is. But throughout the Bible story, it acts as an essential structure for human thriving, priestly service, and kingdom mission.

This leads us back to Israel's priests. As exiles in the Promised Land, they became a sign. Their unique, set-apart way of life pointed to the future "landlessness" of Israel and the church. Such landlessness was not incidental. It was and remains central to God's wider geographic strategy for his chosen people. From a territorial perspective, God's plan for his people unfolds in three stages.[13]

1. God's people must first become a numerous people with a distinct identity. This process began when Abraham and Sarah left a prominent Babylonian city and migrated to Palestine. They and their descendants struggled to gain a foothold for themselves there. But they grew in number after a famine forced them to relocate to Egypt. Though the Egyptians eventually enslaved them, the Israelites multiplied exponentially over a period of four hundred years.

2. God's numerous people must then grow into a distinct identity that reflects God's intentions for all creation. So, immediately after delivering them from Egypt, God equipped his people with Torah. These instructions were designed to align Israel's communal life with the grain of the universe—God's ultimate design for human thriving. God then situated his people in the land of Canaan precisely so they might become a Torah-formed people who could serve as a light to all nations.

---

12. James W. Thompson applies 1 Peter's exilic instructions to churches today in *The Church in Exile: God's Counterculture in a Non-Christian World*, rev. ed. (Abilene, TX: Leafwood Publishers, 2010).

13. Cf. Nugent, *Politics of Yahweh*, 120, where I first develop these phases.

3. Once God's people become a numerous people with a distinct identity reflecting God's intentions for all creation, they must scatter throughout the world. Such exilic scattering was necessary for them to bless all nations, spanning seven continents. It began in earnest with the sixth-century Babylonian exile, which many Jews assumed was temporary. They thought the Messiah would bring them all back to Palestine where they would become a powerful worldly kingdom. They would not go to the nations; the nations would come to them. Yet Jesus had other plans. After completing their training, he commissioned his followers to go into all nations, proclaiming the gospel and making disciples in Jerusalem, then Judea, then Samaria, and ultimately the ends of the earth.

In retrospect, we see that the church's exilic posture was not a last-ditch effort on God's part, as if to salvage an Israelite plan that went sideways. Rather, our resident alien status was hardwired into God's plan for his chosen people from the beginning. It found ultimate fulfillment when he sent Israel's Messiah to gather, equip, and send forth his people in mission. As a church, we therefore embrace our exilic posture as a divine gift. It is *our* priestly inheritance. It represents neither a concession to Israel's disobedience nor a liability to overcome. It is the required posture for fulfilling God's mission, God's way.

The exilic status that the church shares with Israel's priests helps establish the priestly image as a fitting model for framing church-world relations. The church's relationship to the world is certainly more akin to how priests related to their host tribes than how kings related to their subjects or servants to their masters. This correlation has important implications for how the church relates to God and world. And it offers key insights into the nature of the church's life together.

RELATING TO GOD AND WORLD

Exilic living means relating to God and world in specific ways. Exile was not simply a matter of geography. It was a statement of faith that all lands belong to God. Even when they lived in the Promised Land, God's people were aliens and tenants on God's property.[14] The Babylonian exile did not

---

14. Lev 25:23.

fundamentally change this. The Promised Land was God's land before exile and God's land afterward. But middle management changed. Under Torah, middle management belonged to a plurality of leaders among Israel's tribes. God's people later entrusted that power into the hands of a king. From exile forward, however, middle management belonged to foreign nations, and the Israelites had to adjust to their oversight, permanently.

The land would still have a human ruler, but that ruler would not be one of God's people. Someone else would determine what laws would govern all the land's inhabitants. Someone else would protect their borders from foreign invasion. Someone else would control the broad-ranging economic factors that affect the whole region. God's people had to trust God to oversee his chosen middle managers. They had to trust God to supply the basic needs of his people and everyone else through various rulers of the nations where they lived. This new and lasting reality enables God's people now—like Israel's priests back then—to remain relatively impartial when it comes to matters of national governance. We possess a kind of objectivity that enables us to perceive problems and possibilities that fully vested citizens with fixed allegiances to specific political entities lack eyes to see.

Exilic living requires God's people to adopt a priestly servant posture wherever they live. I say "priestly servant" rather than simply "servant" because we are not servants of the rulers of the land, but servants of God, who has given us a peculiar kind of service to render on behalf of our neighbors in every land. God's people serve much like ambassadors, a designation used by the apostle Paul (2 Cor 5:20). Though ambassadors live in foreign territory, they represent their own nation in how they interact with and serve their host nations. Elsewhere, Paul notes that "our citizenship is in heaven" (Phil 3:20) even though we dwell among various nations on earth. The meaning is much the same: we are ambassadors who represent the supranational kingdom of heaven.

Belonging to and representing God's kingdom certainly has its advantages. But its scope is limited. Though God owns all lands, he appoints others to manage them. In particular, he entrusts them to various rulers and authorities, and he asks his people to accept this reality and not rebel against it. Governors exist to serve the common good, but they do so quite differently from God's priestly people. God's people do not rule as kings or as anything else, and that's a good thing. It provides a certain kind of freedom. Since Israel's priests didn't own or rule any tribal territory, they were free to perform other important tasks. They studied Torah, welcomed slayers into their camp, cared for the tabernacle, offered instruction, and led public worship, among other responsibilities.[15]

Through the Great Commission, Jesus has made exiles of all of his disciples, so we need not run the world. This allows us to serve the world with gospel resources that only we possess. Only we can embrace, display, and proclaim God's kingdom in all things. This is an all-encompassing task that demands most of our time, energy, and resources. Attempting to run the world instead is absurd. It's like a gifted musician leaving the stage, only to begin controlling the lights and sound. Someone needs to dim the lights and cue the mics, but professional musicians cannot be replaced in their specific roles. They are most valuable when they do what no one else can. If they don't perform their role, no crowd will fill the seats, and the need for sound and light technicians will have disappeared. And so it is with the church.[16] Rulers and authorities keep the lights on and the mics live so the world may *see* the church displaying God's kingdom and *hear* our invitation to repent and receive the gospel as God's gift.

The church's priestly servant posture serves as neither a curse nor a demotion, but an honor. God's strategy in this world has always required this posture. For the priestly servant posture, God called Abraham out of Babylon and the Israelites out of Egypt rather than confiscate and utilize their domineering imperial resources. It is why God made no provisions in Torah for Israel to have a powerful military presence. It is why the monarchy failed, dispersion followed, and all rebuilding remained modest. It is why God sent the Messiah to a poor family from a small town. He could have chosen a rich family from a booming metropolis. It is why Jesus called an unimpressive group of disciples to follow him. It is why he taught them not to lord over people but to serve them. A priestly servant posture appears weak, but we dare not mistake it for weakness. It is the strength of the divine king working through his lowly people to advance salvation history. It is the power at work in Jesus, the apostles, and the early church. The world may not recognize its superior strength, but God's people confess in faith its truth, relevance, and ultimate triumph.

---

15. I discuss this at length in ch. 5.

16. I am indebted to John Howard Yoder for this analogy in *Discipleship as Political Responsibility*, translated by Timothy J. Geddert (Scottdale, PA: Herald Press, 2003), 44–45.

IMPLICATIONS FOR THE CHURCH

The church's priestly exile calls us to a particular way of life wherever we may live. I call it "light living." It shows up in Scripture in five practical ways that pertain to the church. For each way, I describe what light living entails and provide several examples of what it might look like in action.

Light Locality

When it comes to location, an exilic church needs to remain open and flexibly adaptive to where God's Spirit might lead, "for all who are led by the Spirit of God are children of God" (Rom 8:14). A defining attribute of God's Spirit is that it is not geographically constrained. This is the whole point of Ezekiel's awe-inspiring vision of God's holy mobile throne (Ezek 1–3). Ezekiel saw beneath this throne four sets of wheels intersecting wheels covered with all-seeing eyes. Awesome multi-winged creatures whose heads have multiple faces pointing in all directions hover above the wheels. The Spirit of these hyper-mobile creatures animates the omnidirectional wheels because God's glorious presence cannot be confined to any single place—not even his holy temple in the holy city of the holy land of Israel.

Jesus compares God's Spirit to wind, saying, "The wind blows where it chooses, and you hear the sound of it, but you do not know where it comes from or where it goes. So it is with everyone who is born of the Spirit" (John 3:8). That last part warrants special notice: "So it is with everyone who is born of the Spirit."[17] God is on the move and he calls *his exilic people* to move with him, both individually and collectively. I remember a sermon in which theologian Phil Kenneson compared the Christian life to a sailboat.[18] These are engineered to be propelled by the wind. But one must put the sail up for the wind to catch and carry the vessel along. If we truly wish to be led by God's Spirit, as individuals and as churches, we must pull up the worldly anchors that weigh us down and weave into our lives a rich tapestry of kingdom initiatives. This tapestry serves as the sail that the Spirit blows in kingdom directions.

---

17. Interestingly, the word for "wind" in this passage (and in the language Jesus spoke) is the same as the word for "spirit," as well as the "breath" of life that comes from God.

18. Philip D. Kenneson wrote an insightful book on the Holy Spirit entitled *Life on the Vine: Cultivating the Fruit of the Spirit* (Downers Grove, IL: InterVarsity Press, 1999).

Exiles are not pinned down like those who prize permanent residency. They are not so entrenched that new movements engender fear. Maintaining light locality means that God's people should avoid establishing roots that we are not willing or able to pull up. That may mean avoiding long-term job commitments that tie us to a specific city. It may mean not committing to mortgages that bind us to a particular house indefinitely. Some parents may need to give up the dream of having all their children live close by for the rest of their lives. We should probably also resist the notion of the perfect house in the perfect location, which once realized saddles us with the burden that we must never leave it.

We should not reduce light locality to a negative, legalistic set of prohibitions. Rather we should seek out exciting ways God's Spirit might call us to migrate to new places that maximize our kingdom life and witness. We should seek out kingdom locations to live. That could mean relocating to "mission fields" in other countries. It could also mean couch surfing like Jesus who had "nowhere to lay his head" (Matt 8:20) and who relied on the hospitality of others so he could focus on proclaiming the gospel to more towns. Indeed, it continues to mean these types of things for some, and those who embrace it should receive great encouragement, enthusiasm, and financial support from their church families.

But, biblically speaking, it's not for everyone. It wasn't for Mary, Martha, and Lazarus. Yet even believers who never leave their birth state must seek out kingdom spaces to inhabit. They might consider moving closer to fellow believers so they can more easily share resources, care for one another's children, carpool to common activities, gather to read Scripture, eat meals together, celebrate and commiserate with one another, and simply enjoy regular fellowship. Many people fail to experience true kingdom life because they have settled into a home, neighborhood, or school district that checks all sorts of personal preference boxes but positions them so far away from church family that any true sense of life together is logistically prohibitive.

Light locality should also free congregations to go to the places where the Spirit is calling them to meet needs. The proximity that makes regular fellowship with believers possible also makes kingdom witness to unbelievers possible. Many churches struggle with racial and economic homogeneity. Yet their meeting spaces are often nowhere near the demographic they say they desire to reach for Christ. Or perhaps their facilities exist in the right place, but most of their members reside in neighborhoods exceedingly far away. Our mission statements and Facebook posts appear quite progressive, but not so much our zip codes. Perhaps we need consistent reminders that we exist, in fact, as exiles. Once this reality truly sinks in, it might just free us to make bold moves to bountiful fields that lie ripe for kingdom harvesting.

Light locality does not mean disengagement from the places we live and work or the people we routinely serve. Being fully and faithfully present right where we live does not contradict being ready to move as the Spirit leads. We don't get a sense from Scripture that Jesus or Paul were anything less than "all in" wherever they went, regardless of how long they expected to remain. Quite the opposite, an acute awareness of the shortness of their time together seems to have encouraged them to engage their temporary locations with greater intensity.

God doesn't always call his people to move, and he seldom calls *all* his people to move. But he propelled them from the Promised Land precisely so they would plant and sustain kingdom communities all over the globe. He wants his people to grow and spread out. Jesus initiated not just a new Exodus, but a new Genesis—multiplying and filling the earth with new creation.[19] This is the nature of our exilic priestly mission. It's how all the world gains exposure to God's new kingdom order, which has begun to replace the old. This means that Christians must go to all territories and spread out within each territory in fully present and highly impactful ways.[20]

Light Planning

Sitting loose geographically could be mistaken for glorifying the kind of noncommittal hypermobility that typifies modern Western individualism. More and more, people are choosing not to settle down in a particular place or even with a particular person. They wish to maximize personal freedom to pursue whatever new and exciting opportunity may come their way and somehow complete them. Jesus does not call his followers to that kind of light living. We must consider a second dimension of priestly life, which I call light planning. James, the brother of Jesus, captures it best:

---

19. Gen 1:22, 28; and 9:1.

20. For a rich account of missional engagement in the places where we live, see David E. Fitch, *Faithful Presence: Seven Disciplines that Shape the Church for Mission* (Downers Grove, IL: InterVarsity Press, 2016).

> Come now, you who say, "Today or tomorrow we will go to such and such a town and spend a year there, doing business and making money." Yet you do not even know what tomorrow will bring. What is your life? For you are a mist that appears for a little while and then vanishes. Instead you ought to say, "If the Lord wishes, we will live and do this or that." (Jas 4:13–15)

James knows that God's Spirit is not the only wind that can fill our sails. A spirit of restlessness or discontentment can just as easily blow us to and fro. In the same way, a spirit of escapism, acquisitiveness, utter independence, fear of intimacy, enslavement to trends, or greener pastures can drive us. James warns fellow believers that light living in Christ serves only one purpose: remaining free to do God's will.

Living lightly requires God's people to sit loose on future plans. The church's future has always rested in God's hands. Since we cannot see all that God sees, our plans should always remain tentative. Constrained as we are by sinfulness and finitude, we seldom know what doors will soon open or close. God's ways will always transcend ours because he is managing a sprawling global church, a broken system of powers and principalities, and a seven-continent world with endless needs and opportunities. He wants to use his people to serve his kingdom purposes for this vast world. He wants us to go where he sends and to do what he wants with our specific gifts and resources. And if we won't go, he'll send someone else.

Sometimes we go overboard in our planning in a sincere effort to be responsible. Other times, we overplan to mask our worries and anxieties because we don't really trust in God's provision. Jesus identifies and redirects such lack of faith: "Do not worry, saying, 'What will we eat?' or 'What will we drink?' or 'What will we wear?' For it is the Gentiles who strive for all these things; and indeed your heavenly Father knows that you need all these things. But strive first for the kingdom of God and his righteousness, and all these things will be given to you as well" (Matt 6:25–33).

If we commit to seeking God's kingdom above all, then any plans we make should only be our best attempt to avail ourselves for kingdom service. When a student loses her keys and suspects she dropped them somewhere between her car and dorm room, she heads to the parking lot and begins retracing her steps. But if, on her way, the Resident Supervisor calls to say that someone dropped off keys to the lost and found with her student ID attached, she would quickly abandon her first strategy and head straight to the Supervisor's office. Should it not be the same with us? When God calls us to a specific task that disrupts our prior plans, it is not a disruption at all; it is a necessary recalibration in light of new and more accurate information.

We should make kingdom plans the same way we pursue kingdom locations: guided by God's Spirit. This begins for many with family planning. Christians might pursue singleness as a way of life to free them up as much as possible for kingdom service. Should a Christian choose to marry, their married life should also seek God's kingdom first. This means finding a believing spouse who is eager to prioritize the kingdom with us. It means cultivating a lifelong covenant bond that approximates Christ's love for the church. Occupational plans should also reflect kingdom priorities. What jobs give us the best opportunities to bear witness to God's reign, in ways that our coworkers might find intriguing? What sort of employment frees us up both hourly and financially so we will have plenty of time and resources to be integrally involved in church life—so God can use our love for one another to draw all people to himself? We should also plan vacations with God's kingdom in mind. How might we experience true rest and relaxation that rejuvenates us for continued service? How might we avoid the trap of keeping up with the recreational Joneses in ways that exhaust our energy rather than replenish our reserves?

If we are to become light planners, as far as it depends on us, we will strive to maintain margin in our lives—unplanned or unscheduled time. How can we be available to follow God's Spirit and help a neighbor in need or speak a word from God to someone who needs to hear it when we've booked every slot in our schedule? Thinking ahead is not the problem. The danger comes in treating all of our plans like promises or priorities. Overplanning risks turning "God moments" or kingdom opportunities into unwanted interruptions.

Lasting legacy ambition presents one of the greatest threats to kingdom planning. To find significance in their lives, many goal-driven people strive to build impressive legacies that will endure long after they're gone. That legacy may be an unbeatable record, an enduring organization, a successful business, an impressive building, or a prominent monument with our name on it. Leaving a lasting impact on the world proves tempting for individuals as well as institutions. Of course, there is nothing wrong with making an impact that endures or leading in such a way that what God has entrusted to us is passed along to others after we depart. The potential danger of striving to make a lasting impact is that *longevity itself* can become our goal. When future remembrance becomes our ambition, we typically prioritize only people and opportunities that help us achieve quasi-immortality. People become assets or liabilities to our individual goals, a means to our ends rather than ends in and of themselves.

Perpetuating our own legacy poses additional problems when God wants our particular projects to end with our life. What if it was perfectly suited to our time, but not so much afterward? What if God wishes to build something new and he plans to use our resources as the raw materials? If we truly believe that God gives his Spirit to each member of the body and uniquely gifts each one for specific acts of service on behalf of the body, then we must recognize that even if our occupational endeavor experiences great success, it may not be something God wants others to take up. It may not be something that others are suited to take up—even though it formerly accomplished remarkable things for God's kingdom.

Apart from some sort of divine revelation, how could we possibly know? The prophets and priests of Jeremiah's day kept proclaiming "the temple of the Lord, the temple of the Lord, the temple of the Lord" (Jer 7:4). They could not imagine a world in which God would let this core institution crumble. They could not see themselves being a blessing to the nations without a centralized holy place to which all nations would someday stream. Jeremiah acted as the mouthpiece of God, but the "legacy contingent" considered him a threat to God's mission. They were wrong on all accounts, and Jesus came to the record straight.

If God wants a particular personal or institutional legacy to endure, we can know for sure that God will make sure it does. We won't have to silence dissenters, trample innocents, or fight against powerful momentum that appears to be heading in a different direction. If we must quarrel, coerce, or crush others; if we have to sacrifice our time, peace of mind, or bodies; if we have to neglect our family, churches, or friends; if we find ourselves in constant conflict with kind and godly people—in the course of ensuring that our legacy endures—then it's probably not a legacy that God's mission requires of us.

Few people in Scripture became great because they aspired to greatness. We don't even know the names of those who wrote a good number of our sacred biblical texts. We do know that many who strove to be great were brought low by God. Babel is the namesake of humanity's first run at legacy building.[21] Jesus offers the last word. When his followers kept jockeying for

---

21. Gen 11:1–9.

position and posterity, he instructed them to serve and to sit at the foot of the table. *If* God wants to elevate them, *he* will in *his* timing and *his* way.[22] Followers of Jesus will not strive to build a legacy that bears their own names. Their legacy will be the natural and supernatural fruit of a kingdom-centered life that confesses and exalts only the name of Jesus.

Since the key to kingdom planning is Spirit leading, let us seek the Spirit together. Let us search the Scriptures and pray in the Spirit, asking only to discern God's will. Let us plan and pray as Jesus taught us: "Thy kingdom come, thy will be done."

Light Alliances

Israel's priests never quite fit in. Exiles never truly do. They recognized clearly that they stood out from their host tribes. I'm sure they felt somewhat at home in their designated towns, but they could never be full-fledged tribal members. They couldn't join every cause that motivated their non-Levitical neighbors. They couldn't fight their battles, serve as elders, or start thriving businesses. In like manner, Jesus knew his followers wouldn't fit in and would even be rejected by the world. For this reason, he prayed for divine protection and provision, saying,

> I have given them your word, and the world has hated them because they do not belong to the world, just as I do not belong to the world. I am not asking you to take them out of the world, but I ask you to protect them from the evil one. They do not belong to the world, just as I do not belong to the world. Sanctify them in the truth; your word is truth. (John 17:14–17)

Jesus doesn't ask the Father to help his disciples fit in better; he prays for God to sanctify them—to set them apart as misfits who stay true to God's word.

This holy separation means that certain partnerships and alliances remain off limits for believers. The apostle Paul explains:

> Do not be mismatched with unbelievers. For what partnership is there between righteousness and lawlessness? Or what fellowship is there between light and darkness? What agreement does Christ have with

---

22. Luke 14:7–11.

Beliar? Or what does a believer share with an unbeliever? What agreement has the temple of God with idols? For we are the temple of the living God; as God said, "I will live in them and walk among them, and I will be their God, and they shall be my people. Therefore come out from them, and be separate from them, says the Lord, and touch nothing unclean; then I will welcome you, and I will be your father, and you shall be my sons and daughters, says the Lord Almighty." (2 Cor 6:14–18) ·

Paul said this precisely because certain worldly partnerships were pitting believers against fellow believers. A contextual reading suggests that worldly ideas had crept into the church and poisoned the Corinthians against fellow disciples who labored tirelessly on their behalf. I doubt these worldly ideas were blatant moral offenses like murder, pederasty, or theft. They were probably more subtle and respectable than that. Why else would believers be drawn to them? They were the kind of ideas that entice only some of God's people and then drive a wedge between them and other believers.

In our day, worldly alliances continue to divide the church. We must diligently identify and repent of them. Partnerships with different parties who strive to govern society or implement their vision of social betterment prove most problematic. Some believe strongly that a specific political party best serves the wider public and, on account of this and their love for the world, they willingly disparage Christians with different political leanings. Our convictions about the common good may be spot on, but when they drive us to belittle brothers and sisters in Christ "for whom Christ died,"[23] it is quite possible that we love the world more than God's kingdom.

We are equally susceptible to allying ourselves too closely with a particular hobby, show, sports team, or even exercise routine. Recreational pursuits can be good gifts from God and prime occasions for fellowship and witness, but they must never hinder utmost devotion to God's kingdom work. When we have little time to worship, help a believer in need, or demonstrate God's love to a neighbor but plenty of time to binge Netflix and news feeds, catch all the big games, and finely tune every muscle in our body, something is clearly amiss. Light living calls Christian exiles to keep pastimes in their proper place. Properly ordered, such activities may supplement and enrich a kingdom-centered life, but they can hardly stand at the center—especially at the expense

---

23. Cf. 1 Cor 8:11.

of kingdom witness, fellowship, and love. When such is the case, we should remember the warning of James, the brother of Christ, that "whoever wishes to be a friend of the world becomes an enemy of God" (Jas 4:4).

The most respectful form of worldly allegiance may be our work. Some jobs can be extremely fulfilling, and working long hours can result in significant financial gain and personal satisfaction. Yet such jobs can detract from kingdom service more than enable it. We call this phenomenon "living to work" rather than "working to live." If we are truly committed to seeking God's kingdom above all, it should be obvious to our boss, coworkers, family, and church that the lordship of Christ means more to us than our careers. Jesus says so in clear but sobering terms: "No one can serve two masters; for a slave will either hate the one and love the other, or be devoted to the one and despise the other. You cannot serve God and wealth" (Matt 6:24). Again, we shouldn't assume that Jesus was critiquing an especially heinous form of occupational idolatry. He knew what kinds of alliances routinely tempted good Jewish people back then, and they are probably not so different from those that attract good Christian people today.

Light Leadership

Living lightly requires God's people to forsake all dreams of lording over the lands in which we live. Exiles are seldom expected to seize the reins of societal power, and that is to our advantage. Christ has given us a different vision of power and authority. The servanthood to which he calls us is not a *style* of ruling over people, but an *alternative* to doing so. Light leadership is characterized by service-powered impartiality that seeks the good of all by seeking first God's kingdom.

Since we are neither in control of the world nor under its control, we are perfectly positioned to focus on kingdom concerns and to remain genuinely nonpartisan toward competing factions that vie for world governance. We do so as those who care deeply for this world and who exist precisely for it. Priestly nonalignment positions us perfectly to affirm or critique what is truly good or evil on both sides of society's entrenched antagonisms. What a gift to the world! How refreshing we could be for them. Who else listens to them more genuinely and provides feedback more honestly than those with no interest in joining, co-opting, defeating, or supplanting them? Rather, we strive to encourage the best in all others and to discourage all self-inflicted and other-directed wounds. We lead most profoundly and influence most deeply when we serve others by praying for them and encouraging them to maximize human flourishing in their own service to the common good.[24]

How might election seasons be different if most believers advocated for all parties to receive a fair hearing? Refrained from insults and name-calling? Refused to perpetuate the petty caricatures promulgated by opposing parties? Abstained from all political rancor? Highlighted venues of truly civil discourse? Reminded people that no legislation will fix all that ails society or permanently ruin it? Settled people's fears with historical awareness that the harm inflicted by the current administration will likely be mitigated or reversed by the next one?

What if we stood out for unparalleled patience with imperfect people and processes that take time? Could not such patience expose partisan pundits for being agents of destruction and discord? It might just deprive the fires of friction of much-needed fuel. It may even incentivize politicians and news-casters to rise above the fray. What an opportunity for the church to be salt and light—to genuinely contribute to the peace and civility of wider society.

Likewise, how might wars be different? Or pandemics, humanitarian crises, and economic downturns? The presence of impartial priestly servants is always invaluable. We will stand among the few who see through all the posturing and profiteering and may therefore draw attention to the core issues being overlooked. We won't wait to see how any "side" chooses to frame or spin the situation to their own advantage. We will lead the way in champi-oning the well-being of all parties involved, especially the most vulnerable and the enemy, regardless of which side stands to gain the most politically.

Impartial service is contagious and convicting. Jesus empowered us for light leadership when he called us to turn the other cheek, surrender our clothing, and walk an extra mile.[25] Paul framed it in terms of overcoming evil with good.[26] Both led an infectious movement that continues to make a lasting impact. Their light leadership proved so powerful that we still look to them for direction! The same could not be said of their partisan peers, whether the Herodians, Sadducees, or Zealots. Both Jesus and Paul traded short-term success and limited control for long-term significance in God's eternal kingdom.

24. Cf. 1 Tim 2:1–4.
25. Matt 5:38–42.
26. Rom 12:21.

Light leadership must be practiced and modeled in the body of Christ. Believers should avoid all dog-eat-dog ladder climbing. We should not covet postures of top-down power that permit us to force our will upon others, even when we believe our ideas are in their best interest. Church leaders must devote themselves to activating, elevating, and highlighting the gifts and abilities of others. They should strive to solicit input from everyone, for God gives his Spirit to each member and might speak through any one of us. For this reason, Peter instructs elders, "Do not lord it over those in your charge, but be examples to the flock" (1 Pet 5:3). Lording over seldom looks like oppressive tyranny. More often, we lord over others by monopolizing conversations, controlling outcomes, ignoring voices, deciding unilaterally, and bypassing dissenters. If churches don't display kingdom equality in our structures and practices, we neglect a key aspect of our witness—an aspect that a world weary of being manipulated by those who are hungry for power desperately needs to see.

Light leadership should translate seamlessly into the workforce. Believers need to pay the bills like everyone else, and jobs usually afford us constant contact with unbelievers. Our kingdom commitments should, therefore, constantly be on display. Most work sites maintain highly visible pecking orders with bosses, supervisors, peers, and "inferiors." Salaries and prestige are tied to one's position within this hierarchy. Ladder climbing is therefore expected, if not encouraged. Yet on whatever rung believers find themselves—whether near the top or bottom—we remain children of God and kingdom ambassadors. We represent the lordship of Christ, and he remains our example. As such, we will not covet positions of power that clearly belong to others. We will not belittle others in an effort to elevate ourselves. We will not reduce our peers to competitors for limited promotions and scarce resources. Instead, we will content ourselves with what we have received. We will steward that gift with excellence befitting the God we profess. We will not jockey for positions that may be given to others, though we will humbly accept a promotion that serves our kingdom calling. We will aspire to safeguard the dignity of any we are asked to manage. We will empower them to excel in their service so they may both enjoy their labor and grow in their ability to handle more responsibility. As priestly exiles, we will lead lightly as agents of peace and impartiality. Though our jobs occupy a good deal of our time, the kingdom remains our primary vocation and permeates every aspect of our labor.

Light Possessions

Living lightly means recognizing that our daily bread comes from God. Like scattered Levites who could never become stakeholders in the land, we depend in many ways on the economic productivity and oversight of others. Seeking first God's kingdom means that we do not live to make money or accumulate possessions. Jesus showed that we can do just as well, even better without them. This means avoiding jobs that profit at the expense of others, contribute to the degradation of society, compromise kingdom values, or monopolize our own time and energy. Such avoidance will limit our money-making potential. The highest paying jobs are typically reserved for those who place the company above all else. Like God's kingdom, bosses desire flexibility on the part of their employees—on call all the time and willing to do whatever it takes.

Priestly exiles operate within God's kingdom economy. Though we are subject to the same market forces as our unbelieving neighbors and while we pay the same taxes and shop at many of the same stores, we think quite differently about money and possessions. The church is itself an economic ecosystem—an ecosystem that should point to the abundant economy of God's coming kingdom. In God's kingdom, no one goes without, no one thrives at the expense of others, and no one enjoys the fruit of what their labor alone produces. Rather, in God's kingdom everyone embraces economic interdependence as a gift and contributes in whatever ways they are uniquely suited. No one falters under the weight of crippling debt or sows their excess to the wind. We recognize that all things belong to a God who wants all his children to flourish. No one treats wealth and possessions in a purely private way. Through our excess, God compensates for the deficit of others. Our lack fulfills the need of others, enabling them to give of their bounty so they, too, may participate in our Lord's life-giving generosity.[27]

Sharing is the prevailing currency of exilic economics, and stockpiling is its antithesis. This is why the wealthy struggle to enter God's kingdom.[28] The more one accumulates, the more one is tempted to hoard for oneself and one's progeny. The apostle Paul equated greed with idolatry and listed it among vices like fornication, impurity, and evil desires.[29] Here I submit five guidelines to

---

27. E.g., 2 Cor 8:13–15.
28. Matt 19:24.
29. Col 3:5.

assist God's people as they seek to discern what light possessions might look like in their lives and in the church. This list is far from comprehensive but should help get the conversation started.

First, we should avoid possessing what we are not willing to hold loosely. If owning a particular item—whether a car, house, computer, or coffee maker—causes us anxiety, then it is probably weighing us down in ways that are counterproductive to kingdom witness. In light of the coming kingdom, the apostle Paul recommended a hands off approach, saying, "the appointed time has grown short; from now on, let . . . those who buy [do so] as though they had no possessions, and those who deal with the world as though they had no dealings with it. For the present form of this world is passing away" (1 Cor 7:29–31).

Second, we should avoid possessing what we are not willing to share with others. This relates to the first guideline. Some people experience peace about owning a particular car or house for themselves, but they could not imagine making it available for others. Some have no qualms with caring for an antique car, but they balk at the thought of just anyone riding in it. Some habitually buy things to be used only by their family and closest friends, but not by the people of God or a neighbor in need. Such a tight-fisted approach to possessions risks the idolatry of greed.

Third, we should avoid possessing that which is unfit for serving God's kingdom. If listening to our music, watching our movie collection, or playing our video games in the presence of godly people makes us uncomfortable, they are not likely possessions that truly enrich our lives. This may matter more than we think, for a real connection exists between who a person is and what they choose to own. Jesus affirmed this connection, saying, "where your treasure is, there your heart will be also" (Matt 6:21).

Fourth, we should avoid possessing that which will inevitably possess us. If owning a big screen TV or the latest gaming console will likely monopolize most of our free time and hinder our willingness to volunteer when help or fellowship with the kingdom community is needed, then it likely possesses a stronger grip on us than we do on it. If, on the other hand, those same resources serve as catalysts for fellowship and tools for outreach, they may be exactly the kind of things we should acquire. The same may be said of a phone, boat, pool, trailer, or cabin.

Fifth, we should avoid possessing what we cannot afford. Debt often has a debilitating effect on people's lives. We should certainly avoid frivolous debt.

Still, many Christians walk right into it, even for noble-sounding reasons. We often covet the gift of giving. We want to be the generous person who gives expensive gifts and picks up everyone's check. We want the decked-out entertainment room that everyone piles into for a movie marathon. We want a big truck that can haul just about anything. When we cannot afford such things but purchase them anyway, we saddle ourselves with a burden that robs us of the chance to become the generous people we aspire to be. That debt can lead us to stop tithing or reduce our chances of developing such a habit. Like modern-day Pharisees, our generosity looks sweet on the outside, but is rotten at the core.

If we want to live lightly, we should avoid possessing what we can't afford, as well as what we are unwilling to share, give away, or leave behind as God calls us forth in mission. One might read the preceding paragraphs as a legalistic screed of shoulds and should nots, but this frames the concept incorrectly. The point is that Christ truly came to set us free and give us abundant life.[30] The light living he offers us is best captured by his own words: "Come to me, all you that are weary and are carrying heavy burdens, and I will give you rest. Take my yoke upon you, and learn from me; for I am gentle and humble in heart, and you will find rest for your souls. For my yoke is easy, and my burden is light" (Matt 11:28–30).

Christ calls his priestly exiles to a truly cosmopolitan adventure. Collectively, we get to learn every language, scale every mountain, cross every sea, and settle in every city, suburb, and hamlet. No culture or climate is above or below our purview. We've been commissioned and equipped to incarnate God's kingdom in every context. What a blessing! We couldn't accept such a call if we weren't exiles. We couldn't embrace this opportunity had Christ not divested us of provincial ambitions. His promise to Peter remains open to us: "Truly I tell you, there is no one who has left house or wife or brothers or parents or children, for the sake of the kingdom of God, who will not get back very much more in this age, and in the age to come eternal life" (Luke 18:28–30).

---

30. Cf. Gal 5:1 and John 10:10.

CHAPTER FIVE

Risking Hospitality

PRIESTLY LEGACY

Perhaps no aspect of priestly responsibility is more overlooked than their calling to extend risky hospitality to slayers on the run. I suspect I know why. This function is merely legislated in Numbers and Joshua. We never actually see it in action. We have no story to cement this law into our memories. Nonetheless, this priestly responsibility serves as a powerful image of how God's people today might relate to the wider world. To fully appreciate priestly hospitality, we must understand the precise nature of the problem that such hospitality solved. Doing so takes us back to the primordial violence that wreaked havoc upon the earth.

Once sin entered the world, violence soon followed and quickly escalated. Cain kills Abel whose spilled blood cries out from the ground.[1] God responds by banishing Cain from the soil, the source of his livelihood. Cain worries that during his forced wandering, no one will offer him refuge. Instead, those who hear of his transgression will fear for their own lives and kill him to eliminate the threat. God sympathizes with his concern and places a protective sign on Cain. This sign coincided with God's promise that anyone who kills Cain will face sevenfold vengeance.[2] Though God sought to limit violence with this threat, Lamech, a descendant of Cain, uses it to multiply violence. Having added to the carnage by killing a young man, he vows to avenge

---

1. Gen 4:10.
2. Gen 4:15.

retaliation against himself seventy-sevenfold.[3] After a genealogical interlude, Genesis next portrays the sons of God forcefully taking the daughters of men, perhaps as sex slaves, and likely with the help of mighty warriors.[4] Before long, violence so fills the earth that God elects to destroy it with a flood.[5]

Bloodshed was the most egregious sin to plague God's original creation. Not wishing this trend to continue in a post-flood world, God highlights the sacredness of lifeblood and takes further measures to minimize lethal violence: "For your own lifeblood I will surely require a reckoning: from every animal I will require it and from human beings, each one for the blood of another, I will require a reckoning for human life. Whoever sheds the blood of a human, by a human shall that person's blood be shed; for in his own image God made humankind" (Gen 9:5–6). Blood is sacred to God because the life of people and animals was believed to be in their blood (Lev 17:11).

Since God alone may give and take life, he considers it a grave offense when people take life into their own hands. Human bloodshed also defiles the land, as we saw with Abel's blood crying out from the ground and the floodwaters scrubbing the earth of violence. When God drives the Amorites from Canaan and relocates his own people there, he warns them against defiling the land with violence. He establishes clear protocols to prevent it from happening too often and to make atonement when it does. When someone mortally wounds a neighbor, a fourfold process must be followed to keep things from escalating beyond control, like before the flood.[6]

1. The slayer alone must be killed. The one seeking justice may not touch their family, friends, and possessions. In this context, the saying "life for life" served to limit retaliation, not require it.[7] Only the slayer's blood can atone for the land. Any additional bloodshed would further defile it.
2. The blood of the slayer may only be shed by the nearest kin of the deceased. Though the NRSV refers to this person as the blood "avenger," the term is best translated "redeemer." The point is not so much to punish the offender as to redeem or buy back the sacred

---

3. Gen 4:24.
4. Gen 6:1–4.
5. Gen 6:11, 13.
6. For details about this process, cf. Num 35:16–34.
7. Nugent, *Genesis 1-11*, 142–147.

lifeblood of the deceased. Not just anyone can kill, and there were no professional executioners. Murder is a highly personal act, and the manner of setting things right should be equally personal—not cold and detached.

3. Because someone might falsely accuse someone else of taking a life, at least two witnesses must confirm a deliberate act of bloodshed. The sacredness of life makes it better to allow a true slayer to walk on account of insufficient evidence than to permit the shedding of innocent blood based on false accusations.

4. Since people sometimes kill a neighbor purely by accident, an innocent slayer must be protected by due process. A proper trial must be held, and the blood redeemer must be prevented from killing the slayer until the community has confirmed the slayer's guilt. Israel's priests played a vital role in this process. They were responsible for providing a safe haven for slayers until it was safe for them to return.

As discussed in chapter 8, Levites owned no land of their own. They settled into forty-eight cities scattered among Israel's tribes, six of which were designated "cities of refuge."[8] They served as safe havens while a proper trial was conducted.[9] Should the blood redeemer arrive at their gates and demand the killer's release, the priests must stand firm, protect the killer, and keep the redeemer at bay. When a guilty verdict is reached, priests must then release the slayer to the townspeople to be executed. Should the townspeople fail to conduct a proper trial, the slayer would eventually be released when the high priest dies.[10] Israel's priests played no part in the slayer's trial or execution.

Scripture does not say why priests were chosen for this task. But it was likely because they were uninvolved in tribal governance. They lived as exiles among tribes that they didn't govern. They weren't directly tied to the family who lost a loved one and thus had less reason to bring a suspected killer to premature justice.[11] They neither belonged to their host tribe, judged its cases,

---

8. Num 35:6–7.

9. Josh 20:4–5.

10. Num 35:28.

11. Priests did preside over certain special cases. When someone was killed in the open country and nearby townspeople had no idea who did it, the case was brought before the priests who settled the matter by leading the elders of the closest town through a process of absolution. Such cases underscored the notion that priestly independence

nor executed its criminals. Compared with native tribe members, they had little stake in tribal politics and criminal justice. This enabled them to welcome those whom others feared and shunned. Their relative disentanglement from ordinary civil structures positioned them perfectly to mediate peace.

RELATING TO GOD AND OTHERS

The unique role of priests within Israel resembled Israel's role among the nations. After clearing the Canaanites from the Promised Land, the Israelites held no responsibility for executing God's judgment throughout the world. Though they firmly believed that God actively judged and punished nations,[12] he did not ask them to share this responsibility. Their priestly role was to bless, not to judge. In Isaiah 2, we learn that the Israelites expected the nations to come to them for instruction someday. But even then, they believed that God alone would judge between them. God would broker a lasting peace and transform weapons of warfare into farming equipment (v. 4).

Isaiah 45–49 further explains Israel's hands-off posture toward international judgment. These chapters display God's division of responsibilities. After the destruction of Jerusalem and exile of Israelite leaders, three tasks needed to be completed. Babylon needed to be defeated, Israel needed to be freed from captivity, and God's plan of salvation needed to be shared with the nations. In chapter 45, God appointed Cyrus, a Persian ruler, to carry out the first two tasks. He defeated the Babylonian empire and restored Israel's place in Jerusalem. Cyrus didn't know he was serving God's ultimate purposes, but God used him anyway.[13]

The third and most important task belonged to Abraham's descendants. Isaiah identifies Israel—not Cyrus—as God's chosen servant. Though the Israelites were weak, battered, and unable to save themselves from Babylon, God chose them to be as light to the nations and witness to his salvation.

---

from ordinary tribal politics enabled them to broker peace and grant pardon in ways that transcended ordinary tribal capacities.

12. Cf. Pss 59, 67, 82, and 96.

13. See Isaiah 45:4-5, which corrects simplistic readings of Cyrus's edict (2 Chron 36:22–23). In it, Cyrus claims to be operating at the behest of Israel's God. But this edict should not be over-interpreted. It is likely a form letter that was customized as needed to address every distinct people group that the Persians now governed. Isaiah 45 reminds us that Cyrus didn't know Israel's God any more than the other gods he likely appealed to when soliciting support from other imperial vassals.

Isaiah 49:6 reads, "It is too light a thing that you should be my servant to raise up the tribes of Jacob and to restore the survivors of Israel; I will give you as a light to the nations, that my salvation may reach to the end of the earth." The characteristics that rendered the Israelites unfit for judging the nations made them perfect for spreading good news of salvation.

The same is true for the church. We see this in Jesus's hands-off approach to institutions of judgment. We read about it in Paul's instructions to Christians in Romans 12. Using priestly language, he instructs believers to offer their bodies as living sacrifices that are holy and pleasing to God. To do so, we must not conform to this world but be transformed by the renewing of our minds (vv. 1–3). According to Paul, this renewal entails a distinct way of dealing with enmity. It involves extending hospitality to strangers, blessing and not cursing those who persecute us, living in harmony with others, associating with the lowly, not repaying evil with evil, living peaceably with all, never avenging ourselves but leaving vengeance to God, and supplying our enemies' needs so as to overcome evil with good (vv. 13–21).

The early church didn't think the world would fall apart if they didn't judge wrongdoers. This is not because they weren't able to, being only a small minority. It was because they believed that vengeance belongs to God. They trusted that God has other ways to punish evil and is quite capable of doing so without their help. Their position is evident in Romans 13:1–7 where Paul specifies that God uses governing authorities to punish wrongdoing. Christians can devote themselves to offering God's peace to the wicked because God uses others to keep wickedness in check. Under God's watch, secular authorities keep evil from wreaking too much havoc on wider society. Yet only the love of Christ permanently overcomes such evil, and only Christians commit to such love.

Christians are sometimes tempted to think more highly of ourselves than we should. We presume that if God wants something done, it must be up to us to do it. But that simply isn't true. We are not king of this world; God is. We do not govern the world; God uses powers and principalities to do that. It's not even our job to save the world; God did that through Jesus.

Hear the apostle Paul: "In Christ God was reconciling the world to himself, not counting their trespasses against them, and entrusting *the message* of reconciliation to us. So we are ambassadors for Christ, since God is making his appeal through us" (2 Cor 5:19–20). God did all the saving through Jesus; our role is to inform unbelievers throughout the world that they don't have to live at odds with God and one another. God has already reconciled all of us through Jesus and has appointed his church as ambassadors to represent his victory. We embrace that victory as a gift, display it in our life together, and proclaim it to all who don't know. As Old Testament priests hosted cities of refuge for Israel's most wanted, the Christian church hosts embassies of reconciliation that are open to all.

IMPLICATIONS FOR THE CHURCH

"You have heard that it was said, 'You shall love your neighbor and hate your enemy.' But I say to you, Love your enemies and pray for those who persecute you, so that you may be children of your Father in heaven; for he makes his sun rise on the evil and on the good, and sends rain on the righteous and on the unrighteous" (Matt 5:43–45).

Jesus is not quoting the Old Testament in this verse. No Scripture instructs us to hate our enemies. In fact, God instructs the Israelites to look after their enemies by restoring any of their lost livestock that they might encounter.[14] Rather, Jesus is challenging worldly ideas that had become proverbial Jewish wisdom. He challenged such wisdom not only with words, but with actions. He extended the hand of fellowship to tax collectors (the enemies of Jewish prosperity), Roman soldiers (the enemies of Jewish independence), lepers (the enemies of Jewish purity), prostitutes (the enemies of Jewish families), Samaritans (the enemies of Jewish orthodoxy), and sinners (the enemies of Jewish righteousness).

Though Jesus himself had no home, he offered remarkable hospitality to disreputable people at great risk to his reputation. Our society cannot agree on what constitutes a disreputable person. What counts is determined by whether one supports socially progressive or conservative ideals. Yet the Christian church should stand out in its concern for all who are vulnerable, both socially and financially. This includes undocumented immigrants, ethnic minorities, ex-convicts, refugees, those differently abled, those suffering with mental illness, the poor, the sexually suspect, the minority, and the canceled. The Christian church shares with Jesus and Israel's priests the scandalous responsibility to provide safe havens for societal misfits and rejects. Here I discuss five attributes of the kind of safe havens today's congregations should strive to be.

---

14. Exod 23:4.

Risky Safe Havens

Jesus devoted his earthly ministry to gathering and restoring the Jewish people.[15] He made little effort to reach out to Gentiles. At this point in salvation history, they remained outsiders to the people of God. Only after Jesus ascends and the Spirit descends did the Gentile mission begin. So when Philip and Andrew approached Jesus toward the end of his ministry to tell him some Gentiles wanted to see him, his response was quite telling:

> The hour has come for the Son of Man to be glorified. Very truly, I tell you, unless a grain of wheat falls into the earth and dies, it remains just a single grain; but if it dies, it bears much fruit. Those who love their life lose it, and those who hate their life in this world will keep it for eternal life. (John 12:23–25)

Jesus was clearly referring to his death, which opened the door to Gentile outsiders, but he quickly applied it to his followers as well. As Jesus died to the exclusivity of his earthly mission, so we must die to tidy lives that achieve relative peace and stability only by keeping all "undesirables" at arm's length. We must lose a life of personal comfort and security achieved by surrounding ourselves only with those who love us and are easy to love. We must open our lives to the outsider, outcast, out of money, out of touch, out of style, and out of their mind. Only then will we bear kingdom fruit.

Churches wishing to be safe havens for kingdom mission must open up to unexpected and under-appreciated others. This acceptance begins with *open worship*. When God's people gather for instruction, prayer, praise, and fellowship, we must remain open to any whom God may bring our way. All guests should feel genuinely welcomed into our midst. They might not understand everything we do and why we do it, but they should leave with a profound sense that these Jesus people were surprisingly glad they showed up and genuinely eager to see them return. We should not leave such hospitality to paid staff and volunteer greeters. Guests often judge our hospitality by the vibes they pick up from those they walk by, sit near, and make eye contact with. They will likely care more about our desire to know them than our canned efforts to be known by them. We shouldn't settle for being a church

---

15. Matt 15:21–28.

with a well-trained team of welcoming people; we should aspire to be a truly welcoming church.

Open worship should lead to *open lives*. It's important to welcome the poor, alien, and sinful into our safe public spaces, but that's really just a start. Public gatherings function like the front porches of our homes. They are highly visible and easy to access, but most of our home life takes place inside, around the table, and in the living room. In these places we eat, talk, laugh, and play with friends and family. God wants us to welcome outsiders and outcasts into his family—a family whose life together provides a foretaste of his kingdom. We must truly desire to be welcoming and not do so out of obligation or guilt. Such hospitality may feel uncomfortable and involves risk. Jesus meant it when he said that following him means losing our lives and dying to our old selves. Hosting slayers could not have been easy for Israel's priests. They, too, had spouses, children, and prized possessions. This thought unsettles those who love their lives just the way they are. But while we were still sinners, Jesus welcomed us into his family, and he asks us to do the same for others.

The willingness to welcome strangers and refugees into our lives makes little difference if we lack *open schedules*. For many believers, desire is not the enemy of hospitality; time is. We have so strictly regimented our lives that we have difficulty fitting others into them. God's Spirit often prompts us to reach out to this person or to invite that person over for a meal, but we continually put it off because we simply don't have time. Many of us struggle to truly love our families, church friends, and neighbors. How can we make space for potentially high-maintenance strangers? The pace of modern society makes this increasingly difficult. It's hard to keep up with our jobs, chores, exercise routines, current events, and social media feeds, while freeing up a little time to relax and replenish our energy. Life does not offer easy answers to this dilemma, but God has given us all the time we need to carry out his kingdom mission. To see our time clearly, we might begin by taking a detailed inventory of how we spend our time. Then we can invite fellow believers to help us imagine creative ways to devote *all* of our time to kingdom witness.

Despite our shortcomings, God usually finds ways to bring strangers into our midst. In fact, the stranger people are the more likely they are to be patient with us. The lonely and broken have often received much grace and are eager to extend it to others. As we incorporate them into our lives, we should make sure they have *open opportunities* to serve. We must be careful not to consign them to a class of needy people who always seem to be on the receiving end. How might they use their unique gifts and perspectives? How might they experience the truth of Christ that giving is more blessed than receiving? Only then will they feel like true members of the body of Christ.

Risky safe havens attract risky people. Churches committed to integrating them give the Spirit ample reason to send more their way. Praise be to God! Yet those who participate in such ministry will find themselves quite busy and susceptible to burnout. The adage rings true that "hurt people hurt people." Safe havens must, therefore, commit to *open communication*. Who needs help? Who needs a break? Who is being neglected? Who is taking advantage of whom? The body of Christ must talk together on a regular basis.[16] Some people need to talk things through. Others just need to be heard. Many of us routinely go about things the wrong way and need fresh perspectives and godly counsel. When we gather to discern God's will, the Spirit of Christ enters our midst and guides us into truth.[17] And when we ask for kingdom things, God eagerly supplies our need.[18]

Disentangled Safe Havens

Risky hospitality seems counterintuitive. Shouldn't sinners suffer the negative consequences of their poor decisions? Shouldn't poor people get jobs? Shouldn't mentally ill people get psychiatric help? Shouldn't social service agencies handle these sorts of things? Wouldn't the world be better off if someone just toppled dictator X? Good citizens ask questions like these. They pay their taxes so civil servants can meet social needs, take bad people off the streets, and remove corrupt people from power. But exiles don't think this way. They, too, live as aliens. They don't belong to the world system, and they don't expect it to supply all their needs. Nor do they presume to have enough clout or influence to make things happen on the national scene. Exiles stick together so their own people don't slip through the cracks. They remain sympathetically disposed and perfectly positioned to welcome others who don't quite fit in or are perceived as a threat.

---

16. For an excellent practical guide, see C. Christopher Smith, *How the Body of Christ Talks: Recovering the Practice of Conversation in the Church* (Grand Rapids: Brazos, 2019).

17. Matt 18:20; 1 Cor 5:4; and John 16:13.

18. Matt 7:7–11; John 14:11–14; and 1 John 5:14–15.

Christians who make themselves at home in this world tend to be less accepting and more judgmental toward social misfits. If we truly aspire to be safe havens for God's kingdom, we need to remain respectfully disentangled from this world's mechanisms of control, judgment, and prosecution. These processes have their place in God's providential containment of human rebellion, but they're unfit for Christian mission. As disentangled priests, God uses us to do what centralized coercive power cannot do; namely, change hearts and overcome evil with good.

Disentangled safe havens require *separate structures* from the world. Separation of church and state is not just a good Western idea that accommodates widespread lack of faith and keeps religious violence in check. It's the deliberate posture to which God calls his people all throughout Scripture. The church has its own political structure with its own citizenry, global agenda, and federation of diverse constituencies united across space and time. Worldly structures of governance are concerned with either maintaining or advancing the current order of things in a specific provincial space at the present point in time. Their ambition may be conservative or revolutionary, but their means are inherently coercive. Since the church exists to seek first God's kingdom by embracing the way of Christ, displaying it in every nation, and proclaiming it to all people, our structures must be more flexible, peaceful, forgiving, and generous than those of our host nations.

Disentangled safe havens require *separate processes*. God offers his kingdom as a gift. Those who embrace it do so of their own volition. No one is forced to accept the way of Christ, and the option of rejecting it remains available. The church must present God's offer to all, welcome those who accept that offer into our shared life, and hold each other accountable to it as long as we wish to remain in him. We, therefore, maintain our identity and protect our shared mandate through the process laid out concisely in Matthew 18:15–20. We confront those who depart from the way of Christ in a private and respectful manner in hopes that they will repent. Should they refuse, we involve additional parties to help foster reconciliation. If that doesn't work, the whole church appeals to them in love. If they still refuse, the body accepts and recognizes their refusal by confessing that this member no longer wishes to seek first God's kingdom with us. The former member may then live however they wish—independent from us and our shared mission—though we will continue to pray that they would repent and be restored to God and to us. This whole process is quite delicate, personal, and adapted to the specifics of each situation. It would not be possible if the Spirit of Christ were not present and working in our midst (v. 20).[19]

The world possesses little patience for this sort of process and lacks the promise of Christ's empowering presence. They rely mostly on promulgating laws and hoping that the threat of hefty fines, lengthy imprisonment and, in extreme cases, execution will deter most deviant behavior. The church can implement a more gracious process, in part, because the world's measures keep many of the worst offenders and offenses in check. We need not concern ourselves with prosecuting criminals, protecting national borders, fighting wars, or maintaining legal systems that elicit the assent of most citizens. The coercive processes involved in carrying out these tasks have no place among God's people. Our ends are simply incompatible with the world's means.

Disentangled safe havens must also maintain *separate standards*. By this I do not mean that we follow God's ways in all things and the world doesn't, though that is true. I mean that we hold our own people accountable to God's kingdom standards and we don't lay those same expectations on unbelievers. We don't condone their ungodly behavior, but we recognize their God-given ability to reject his kingdom and live as they wish. God will judge their lives in his time and in his way, and he has withheld this responsibility from us. Constantly expressing our disapproval of unbelievers' life choices through public statements or government legislation places us in a needlessly antagonistic relationship with them. It frames us as enemies of freedom rather than embassies of opportunity. Instead, we should set an example for them and offer God's kingdom to them on God's terms: as a gift they may freely accept or reject. Should they express interest in this gift, we will certainly invite them to count the costs of joining us in mission and to consider the kingdom standards that God has set for us. Apart from such interest, however, we should heed Paul's words to the church in Corinth: "What have I to do with judging those outside? Is it not those who are inside that you are to judge? God will judge those outside" (1 Cor 5:12–13).

For churches to remain disentangled—with separate structures, processes, and standards—we must be mindful of forces that could undermine such disentanglement. One such force includes the occupational choices of our members. Christians are well suited to extend risky hospitality to societal misfits precisely because we confess that we, too, are misfits. Our Scriptures, our songs, and our prayers remind us that we would be nothing if not for

---

19. Cf. also 1 Cor 5:4.

the grace of God. They also remind us that God delights in using us for his kingdom purposes precisely because we live as people of little account.[20] Society preaches a different story. It entices us to greatness through wealth, appearance, possessions, positions, and accomplishments. This being the case, the unfiltered gospel comes as something of a shock: first is last, least are great, poor are rich, leaders serve, wisdom is folly. Without constant reminders in worship and rigorous accountability in fellowship, we too would succumb to worldly notions of greatness. High-profile and high-power jobs often undermine or inoculate believers against the transformation required by the gospel. Forty plus hours of weekly conditioning simply overpower the few hours of faith formation that most believers receive.

Even worse, churches routinely nominate people with significant power and prestige in the workplace for positions of leadership in the church. They naïvely hope that successful career folk will be able to leverage occupational success to help churches grow numerically and remain viable financially. The impact of this strategy can be devastating to Christian hospitality, as the community wields worldly wisdom to achieve kingdom ends. This scenario is not merely hypothetical. It has been happening since the first-century church. The book of James was written to a church with this mindset. In chapter 2, we see some members showing blatant favoritism toward wealthy people joining the fellowship at the expense of the poor. James identifies such favoritism as "faith without works," which is dead. He later forbids worldly people from becoming teachers and clearly distinguishes between divine and worldly wisdom (ch. 3). Finally, he warns these believers that greedy rich folk stand condemned and that friendship with the world is enmity with God (ch. 4).

James took the threat of worldly church leadership seriously and we should too. His situation differs little from ministers who favor playing golf with wealthy members over sharing coffee with low-status members. They know who pays the bills, and they show gratitude accordingly. My point is this: formation matters. Hours invested yield a return. If we hope to rise above worldly mechanisms of control, judgment, and prosecution, we would do well to avoid careers that train us in such mechanisms and condition us to process all of reality through them. At the very least, we should come alongside members in high-risk careers and help them imagine creative ways to maintain kingdom standards in all things. We certainly

---

20. 1 Cor 1:26–31.

shouldn't reward those who fail to do so with positions of influence in the Christian community.

Peacemaking Safe Havens

The defining attribute of safe havens is that they are, in fact, safe. Levitical cities of refuge would have been useless had a slayer escaped from a blood redeemer only to find that their priestly hosts were judgmental, suspicious, or hostile to them. Likewise, if the church is to be a safe haven for the poor, outcast, refugee, sinner, hurting, and recovering, then God's people need to be people of peace. Broken people who flee to us are often running from conflict. They desperately need to receive and experience the peace of Christ. "Blessed are the peacemakers," Jesus said, "for they will be called children of God" (Matt 5:9). The body of Christ is not perfect, but it should be a people of peace. As Paul says in Ephesians 2, we are the new humanity, created in Christ who has broken down the wall that separates people, having terminated all hostility on the cross.[21] Christ is our peace, and we extend his peace to all who enter our midst.

Peacemaking seldom comes naturally. It takes formation and practice to undo a lifetime of bad habits that lead to conflict. We have learned to fight, flee, or freeze whenever we feel threatened. Or, we have so little tolerance for discomfort that we have completely walled ourselves off from those who might hurt us. The body of Christ must, therefore, intentionally learn the way of peace. We need to rest so securely in the peace of Christ that we are not threatened by whomever God may lead our way. If we hope to offer peace to strangers and enemies in situations where they may not understand or even desire it, we must first practice peace where it is expected. We must extend peace to one another within the body of Christ. Here I discuss three practices that help us cultivate a culture of peace that befits priestly hospitality.

First, priestly safe havens must commit to *teaching peace*. As we saw in early Genesis, violence is the ugly condition of a fallen world. At its core, the story of Scripture recounts how the God of Israel and Jesus Christ has been waging peace against a violent world. On a relational level, peace means reconciling strained relationships between humans and God, humans and creation, and humans and one another. As a matter of essence, peace means

---

21. Eph 2:11–22.

restoring wholeness to fragmented humanity and cursed creation. Israel's Torah can be summarized as divine instruction in the way of peace in all these areas. Israel's self-effacing autobiography confesses how God's people traded his vision of peace for worldly security and ambition, which eventually led them right back into a world of violence. God then sent his Son to show us the way of peace. Jesus inaugurated Israel's long-awaited peaceful kingdom, after taking all of the world's violence upon himself, putting it to death on the cross and triumphing over it in his resurrection and ascension. Jesus then commissioned his followers to proclaim peace throughout the world. He told them to invite all people into his peaceful kingdom, which will encompass all things when Christ returns to permanently vanquish all violence and death.

Peace is, therefore, no sidebar to Christian identity. It shouldn't be viewed as the special emphasis of Mennonites or the naïve conviction of pacifists. Peace permeates the Bible story. The Messiah taught and exemplified peace. And peace is reinforced in just about every New Testament writing.[22] It stands at the heart of our mission and must be taught rigorously and regularly. As James puts it, "a harvest of righteousness is sown in peace for those who make peace" (Jas 3:18).

Second, followers of Christ must take seriously every opportunity for *practicing peace*. Conflict seems to follow people around like their shadow. We encounter it with disgruntled coworkers, jealous siblings, insecure neighbors, and even fellow believers trying to make a name for themselves. We encounter it in ourselves, as we sometimes initiate or exacerbate the conflict. Our society reflexively crushes our enemies when we possess the upper hand. Or, we lay low and let things blow over when it's not clear who will triumph. Children of God, on the other hand, should view conflicts as valuable opportunities to learn what makes for peace. Most conflicts are grounded in misunderstanding, insecurity, or opportunism. No one-size-fits-all approach will resolve all conflicts. But repeated attempts at making peace in a spirit of gentleness, patience, mercy, and grace gradually hone our instincts, correct our mistakes, and refine our skills.

Peacemaking is not an individual affair. Those who seek peace will experience the work of God's Spirit time and again, which builds our confidence in his continued support. We should also walk alongside brothers and sisters who are experienced in the way of peace. Since Matthew 18 provides our default

---

22. See Appendix 1.

process for seeking peace, we will usually begin with a discrete conversation with the other party to the conflict. More often than not, a frank but gentle conversation will bring resolution. When it doesn't, we should strive to include someone else whom both parties respect and believe may be genuinely helpful in mediating peace. If chosen well, this person will teach us a good deal more about peacemaking.

The process may not end there, as each situation differs considerably. But those committed to facing and resolving conflict biblically will soon find that they have grown in peacemaking and have relatively few enemies and conflictual feelings. Ignoring or avoiding all conflict produces the opposite results. We don't grow in peace, we continue to be embroiled in conflict, and we remain awkwardly at odds with multiple people—many of whom have no significant problem with us, but who remain saddled with enough unresolved issues to leave tension in the relationship. Time may lessen the intensity of our negative feelings, but it never truly liberates us from the bondage of enmity and insecurity. Communities that take opportunities for peacemaking seriously truly become safe havens. They are best positioned to regard risky guests not so much as threats to be avoided but opportunities to demonstrate, practice, and extend the peace of Christ.

A third practice for cultivating a culture of peace entails *supporting peace*. We do so by empowering fellow peacemakers to make tough choices that foster reconciliation. Peacemaking can sometimes be exhausting. Brothers and sisters offer valuable assistance not only by praying for us but by carrying other burdens or responsibilities that we are bearing. Such responsibilities may include childcare, chores, transportation, or volunteer work for the church. Additional help in these areas frees us to devote the time we need to make peace without fear of neglecting other important commitments.

In other circumstances, a financial gift may help resolve a conflict. One party may have offended another by doing something that cost them money, took up their time, or inflicted damage upon some particular possession. Or perhaps a company or contractor wronged us and ended up costing us more than we could afford. When this happens, the family of faith can help us make peace by paying off the debt and eliminating the financial component of the conflict. Relational fallout may still result, but a little bit of money can often mitigate the tension and facilitate easier dialogue.

Sometimes we need emotional support, rather than physical or financial. Conflict can be demoralizing. It may force us to face aspects of our own lives that bring us shame. We may have to turn the other cheek, walk the extra mile, or otherwise give sacrificially of ourselves to overcome evil with good. In such cases, an encouraging conversation, shared meal, or thoughtful note can lift our spirits and embolden us to see the peacemaking process all the way through. This list could go on indefinitely. We could offer one another time away to clear our heads, space in our homes to be still, a favorite beverage to cheer us up, or a Scripture passage that speaks comfort, hope, or truth into our situation. Believers will more likely face conflict head on and make peace when we know that the body of Christ supports us and will do all it can to enable us to do the right thing.

Trusting Safe Havens

Not being in control can be frightening. A few winters ago, I was driving down an icy hill. I remember as if it were yesterday because I had borrowed a friend's car. The inevitable eventually happened. I started sliding out of control and careened straight toward bumper-to-bumper traffic, with no ability to stop or steer my way to safety. I could only brace for impact and trust that God and a bunch of strangers might somehow make a way where I couldn't see one. Thankfully, they did. Like the waters of the Red Sea, the cars in my path parted down the middle and I slid on through without a bump or scratch.

Israel's priests must have felt that way sometimes. As experts in Torah, they knew God's ways better than their host tribes, yet they remained very much at their mercy. Tribal elders made key decisions that controlled the social and economic climate in which everyone lived, including the Levites. And so it is with the church. We barrel through world history, out of control, having to depend on God's providential use of world powers to handle things that affect our wellbeing and mission. As God's exilic people, we must focus on our priestly calling and trust God to take care of everything beyond our purview. Despite all appearances, we must also trust that our modest contributions to world peace truly bear the hope of world history. Sometimes planting and sustaining communities that embrace, display, and proclaim God's kingdom doesn't seem like what this world needs. Detractors within and without won't hesitate to remind us of this. Here I discuss four practices that engender the kind of trust upon which priestly safe havens are built.

The first thing we must do is *read the Bible story*. The author of Hebrews wrote to encourage a struggling, doubting congregation. He challenged them to trust God that the sacrifice of Jesus sufficiently overcame all of their sins, once and for all. They must stop seeking additional practices to atone for ongoing sin. To do so besmirches the blood of Christ and the perfect will of God. After making this case with remarkable ingenuity and clarity, the author rehearses the legacy of Israel's faithful ancestors (culminating in Jesus) and exhorts his readers to imitate their faith (Heb 11).

In each instance, the faithful Israelite heeded God's call in light of his promise that their faithfulness would indeed be enfolded into his ultimate purposes for Israel and world history. To set the stage for this testimony, the Hebrews author epitomizes faith memorably as "the assurance of things hoped for, the conviction of things not seen" (Heb 11:1). God requires no less from us. We must trust that the providential place God has assigned us in world history is, indeed, the best and only way. The Hebrews church doubted whether Jesus's death sufficiently atoned for their sin and sought to supplement it with additional activities. Many in today's church doubt that our priestly commission, paired with God's providential use of world powers, will sufficiently meet this world's needs. They also seek to supplement God's kingdom mission where they find it lacking, in the face of infinite divine wisdom. If we are to trust God in the face of uncertainty, we too must remember the story of God's people and how, in Jesus, he delivered on all his promises.

One does not have to get far into the Bible story to realize that if God's purposes are going to be realized, it will be in God's way and by his power and strength. God seldom works in ways that seem right to us. So we must *pray for faith*. Like the father of a first-century demon-possessed child, we implore Jesus, "I believe; help my unbelief!" (Mark 9:24). Those who pray daily for God's kingdom to come and his will to be done find themselves growing into that reality. Prayer opens our eyes and calibrates our expectations to see God working in our lives and among the family of faith. Failure to pray tends to erode our trust in God. We revert to viewing people and events from a human point of view. Praying for faith involves praying for things that are beyond our control. Paul encourages first-century believers to do this very thing:

> I urge that supplications, prayers, intercessions, and thanksgivings be made for everyone, for kings and all who are in high positions, so that we may lead a quiet and peaceable life in all godliness and dignity. This is right and is acceptable in the sight of God our Savior, who desires

everyone to be saved and to come to the knowledge of the truth. (1 Tim 2:1–4)

This prayer is truly humble. It recognizes a necessary connection between the work of pagan rulers and all people coming to a saving knowledge of Christ. Paul cannot have meant that the Roman rulers would become evangelists who would offer truthful exposition of the gospel. More likely, he realized that the relative and imperfect peace that they accomplish through top-down coercive power enables kingdom communities to flourish and reach out to others through our peaceable godly lives. This prayer offers a middle way between the twin errors of naively striving to use world powers to accomplish our evangelistic task *and* speaking only ill of the powers as if they were nothing but enemies of the gospel. In reality, God uses both worldly kingdoms and the kingdom of Christ to accomplish his saving purposes, though each plays a different part. This, too, requires faith. Lord, we believe; help our unbelief!

Trust requires teaching and prayer, but it also takes practice. One place to begin is to *trust one another.* In many ways, the body of Christ exists as a microcosm of the whole world. God has gifted the body with diverse people who possess diverse gifts. No member can do it all. We all need and depend on each other to fulfill God's purposes for our life together. That's why the apostle Paul instructs us to submit to one another.[23] The interdependence without which our life together could not work mirrors the interdependence between the Levites and their host tribes, and between the church and our host nations.

When exercising, it is easier to start with shorter distances and lighter weights before building our capacity to handle more. So, too, as we learn to trust God's wisdom in forming an interdependent family of faith, we grow to trust his will for our interdependent relationship with world powers. Yet interdependence only truly works if each member does their own part and does not covet or usurp the role of others. Interdependence within the body of Christ works precisely because we are all distinct. Likewise, we must frame our interdependence with governing authorities in terms of respectful disentanglement—remaining unique in our function but appreciating the unique function of the other.[24]

---

23. Eph 5:21.

24. I discuss "respectful disentanglement" from the powers at length in *Endangered Gospel*, ch. 22.

Finally, if we wish to trust God that our role in helping the world centers on faithfulness to kingdom mission and that God has appointed others to take care of what lies beyond our purview, then we must *guard our minds* from taking in a constant stream of false messaging that gradually erodes our trust. This echoes the above discussion about jobs. Only, here I am focusing on how we spend our free time. It might be the shows we watch, music we enjoy, news we digest, podcasts we listen to, or books and magazines we read. Several passages alert us to the reality of such formation and deformation.

- "Do not be conformed to this world, but be transformed by the renewing of your minds, so that you may discern what is the will of God—what is good and acceptable and perfect." (Rom 12:2)
- "Solid food is for the mature, for those whose faculties have been trained by practice to distinguish good from evil." (Heb 5:14)
- "We destroy arguments and every proud obstacle raised up against the knowledge of God, and we take every thought captive to obey Christ." (2 Cor 10:4–5)

These passages focus on the renewal of our minds precisely because our minds are so easily corrupted. They highlight the role of training and practice because repetition wires our mental grid in ways that alter our perception of good and evil. These verses use language of destruction and captivity because we are engaged in a battle for our minds. If we don't take the enemy seriously, we very well may lose on account of our passivity.[25] When it comes to trusting God in all things, taking in a sermon one hour a week falls terribly short. We may have to limit whatever daily mental stimulation we digest that threatens to dilute our confidence in the truth of God's word.

Feasting Safe Havens

No conversation about hospitality would be complete without food. Consider Abraham and Sarah's lavish culinary hospitality to strangers:

[Abraham] looked up and saw three men standing near him. When he saw them, he ran from the tent entrance to meet them, and bowed down to the ground. He said, "My lord, if I find favor with you, do not pass

---

25. See also Eph 6:10–17.

by your servant. Let a little water be brought, and wash your feet, and rest yourselves under the tree. Let me bring a little bread, that you may refresh yourselves, and after that you may pass on—since you have come to your servant." So they said, "Do as you have said." And Abraham hastened into the tent to Sarah, and said, "Make ready quickly three measures of choice flour, knead it, and make cakes." Abraham ran to the herd, and took a calf, tender and good, and gave it to the servant, who hastened to prepare it. (Gen 18:2–7)

It is tempting to dismiss such hospitality as cultural, and to some extent it always is. But Abraham's hospitality also stood in stark contrast to the welcome these same strangers later received from the city of Sodom.[26] Regardless, the author of Hebrews commends such hospitality to the believing community, saying, "Do not neglect to show hospitality to strangers, for by doing that some have entertained angels without knowing it" (Heb 13:2).[27]

Eating is a powerful social practice and Jesus made the most of it. Not all Jewish leaders did so in his day. John the Baptist and the Pharisees were distinguished by their fasting. That's what spiritual people did. Yet people remembered Jesus for feasting.[28] Even after the resurrection, we mostly find Jesus teaching and eating. Two of his followers recognized him only after he had broken bread.[29] This should not surprise us. Jesus came to restore fellowship between humans and God, humans and one another. In a real sense, this restoration begins at the table.

According to today's hyper-individualistic mindset, you are what you eat. But, socially speaking, you are who you eat with. Invitations to break bread are invitations to fellowship. Such invitations communicate acceptance and a desire for friendship. For this reason, people tend to carefully select who they eat with. If I accept or extend invitations to the wrong people, their reputations will rub off on me. I'll get pegged as "one of them." The Jews of Jesus's day were aware of such association and took offense at his table company, grumbling, "This fellow welcomes sinners and eats with them" (Luke 15:2). They're not wrong. Jesus ate with a strikingly diverse spectrum of people, including zealots, fisherman, tax collectors, lepers, Pharisees, and even the

---

26. Gen 19:1–5.
27. See also Rom 12:13.
28. Luke 5:33.
29. Luke 24:30–31.

one who would betray him.[30] Mealtime with Jesus was likely the only time one could find zealots and tax collectors around the same table. Jesus was probably also the only one who could eat with both lepers and Pharisees, the least clean and those most obsessed with purity.

This wasn't just Jesus being Jesus. One could easily write off his example as the unique vocation of the Messiah. He came to die for all people, especially sinners, so welcoming everyone made sense for him. Yet Jesus expected his followers to offer the same uncommon hospitality:

When you give a luncheon or a dinner, do not invite your friends or your brothers or your relatives or rich neighbors, in case they may invite you in return, and you would be repaid. But when you give a banquet, invite the poor, the crippled, the lame, and the blind. And you will be blessed, because they cannot repay you, for you will be repaid at the resurrection of the righteous. (Luke 14:12–14)

Selectivity is a hard habit to break. Even the apostles struggled to make space at the table for Gentiles. It took a dramatic vision to open Peter's eyes to this unsettling reality and, afterward, he still struggled to live it out consistently.[31] Sharing the gospel message with Gentiles proved to be one thing, but sharing a table with them quite another. It is therefore quite significant that Jesus asked his followers to remember him in the breaking of bread. I suspect that he wanted them and us to eat together precisely so we would never forget how he feasted and those with whom he feasted. Eating together provides a continual reminder that our lives, too, should remain perpetually open to the outcast, stranger, and sinner. For we were once strangers to God, and now he has adopted us as children and asked us to welcome all outsiders to his banqueting table.

Christians have neglected the practice of eating together. Many congregations have simply become too big to do so in their facilities.[32] With the rise of small-group ministry, meals have enjoyed a modest comeback. But small-group gatherings tend to be less accessible to strangers and less attended by the kinds of sinners Jesus welcomed. How might we become priestly

30. Luke 5:27–39; 7:36–50; 11:37–54; 14:1–24; 22:14–38; and John 12:1–11.
31. Gal 2:11–14.
32. For an informative history of how the Lord's Supper evolved out of a shared meal around the table and into a brief ritual before an altar, see John Mark Hicks, *Come to the Table: Revisioning the Lord's Supper* (Abilene, TX: Leafwood Publishers, 2002).

safe havens who welcome both friends, strangers, and sinners to our feasts? Though becoming a kingdom community cannot be reduced to a formula, here I suggest four steps that might help us become feasting safe havens worthy of our calling.

1. Recover the practice of sharing full meals together as believers. We don't have to start with all-church meals. We can begin small by hosting whatever size meals our homes can accommodate. If we are not in the habit of eating together as a body, there will be no fellowship meal to which we might invite strangers and sinners.

2. Commit to eating meals with believers who differ from us. If we only eat with likeminded fellow believers whom we enjoy being around, our feasting is no different from the world around us. Such eating does little to form us into people capable of risky hospitality. This was likely the reason Jesus instructed his followers to invite the socially and financially disadvantaged to their banquets.[33]

3. Invite unbelievers to share meals with our families. Many of us have good relationships with unbelievers at work, at school, and in our neighborhoods or apartment buildings. If we start by inviting unbelievers with whom we are comfortable, we can begin developing skills of hospitality that will become second nature to us.

4. Invite unbelievers who push us beyond our comfort zone. By following steps 1–3, we learn how to fellowship with a wide variety of people—those who are like us and those who are different, those who share our faith and those who do not. This prepares us for a kind of risky hospitality that may have seemed difficult or intimidating at first—the kind that Jesus exemplified and challenged his followers to imitate.

These four steps make sense as a logical sequence intended to help those who struggle with risky hospitality. Following that order is strictly optional, but taking all four groups seriously is not. Jesus cast a wide net, and so should we. Taking a deliberate approach to expanding our capacity for hospitality makes no sense if we are not going to use each step as an opportunity to learn. Like most practices at which we become proficient, we must intentionally seek ways

---

33. Luke 14:12–14.

to learn and grow. As my friend Steve likes to remind me, "Practice doesn't make perfect; perfect practice makes perfect." Here I list a few additional practices that are helpful:

- Accept invitations. Being a guest provides an excellent way to learn how to host. Observe what goes well and what goes poorly.
- Consult believers who are gifted in hospitality. God has gifted the body in diverse ways for a reason. When it comes to skills for kingdom service, we don't look to the most skillful just *to do* what they are skilled in, but *to lead* the rest of us to a better understanding and execution of their particular skill.
- Devote time to hospitality. Many of us come home from work somewhat tired and peopled out. We just want to kick off our shoes and relax for the evening. As a result, most people extend few invitations. We get stuck in a rut that is hard to steer out of. So be proactive. Set a goal or even a schedule. Perhaps offer an invitation twice a month or every other Saturday night. If it's worth doing, it's worth planning to do.
- Budget money. Hosting others costs more money than feeding only ourselves. So, when finances are stretched, we can easily talk ourselves out of hosting people. But if we can set apart money in advance as a matter of habit, then we can look forward to spending it in creative hospitable ways. If the budget will simply not allow for hosting others, there are ways to share the financial burden or otherwise be thoughtful with our words, décor, and flatware.
- Plan out some talking points. Conversation often proves to be the most awkward part of sharing meals. We typically spend a good deal of time and energy thinking about what we will eat, what we will wear, and how we'll get the house ready in time. What we will say is just as important, and most of us devote little time to thinking about that in advance. For several years, I shared lunch weekly with an older gentleman also named John. He usually brought a notebook with several thoughts and questions that he hoped to chat about during our time together. I always looked forward to our time together.
- Remember the children. Parents invest more time and energy into their children than just about anything or anyone else. As

guests, they are often nervous about whether their kids will behave. Showing kindness to people's kids provides great relief to them. It makes them less anxious and more engaged in fellowship. Keep children in mind for the food, the activities, and especially the talking points. A little bit of intentionality goes a long way.

- Build common ground. Identity formation in modern society focuses on helping people realize their individuality. We, therefore, assume that people will like us more if we can show them how unique we are. During table talk, we often find ourselves focusing on what we like and don't like, in contrast to others in the room. Yet human emotions are connected to complex chemical reactions that are triggered by external stimuli. As a result, people "feel" better and thus prefer to be around those who like what they like and hate what they hate. So, if you're a cat person, try to restrain your loathing of dogs in front of a dog owner, and vice versa. People hold far greater attachments to their pets than to first- or second-time dinner guests. Differences will surface over time, but when making first impressions and building friendships it's best to lead with common ground.

Anxiety runs rampant in society and in the church, and people are especially anxious about connecting with new people. Feasting together is a time-tested way to build camaraderie. Let us take up Jesus's practice of breaking bread on a regular basis. If we wish to do so in ways that bear witness to God's kingdom, we will need to eat like Jesus—not only with those who are easy to be with, but also with those who are strange to us and perhaps even threatening. And like Jesus, we must not do so from a posture of worldly power, privilege, and establishment. Indeed, as Stanley Hauerwas and Jonathan Tran helpfully remind us, "The church not only welcomes the stranger, but *is* the stranger, constituted as she is entirely by migrants, herself a migrant through the world."[34]

---

34. Stanley Hauerwas and Jonathan Tran, "A Sanctuary Politics: Being the Church in the Time of Trump," ABC Religion and Ethics, March 30, 2017, https://www.abc. net.au/religion/a-sanctuary-politics-being-the-church-in-the-time-of-trump/10095918.

CHAPTER SIX

Stewarding the Sacred

PRIESTLY LEGACY

Because the man Levi took the blood of the Shechemites into his own hands, his descendants were scattered among the Israelites and denied their own portion of the Promised Land. They had to embrace the status of exiles. God turned that curse into a blessing by giving them priestly responsibilities that turned their scattering into an integral component of their priestly vocation. Their landless status among their brothers perfectly suited the Levites to supervise cities of refuge. In addition, God gave a specific branch of Levites exclusive sacrificial duties inside the sanctuary. And he assigned all other Levites the sacred duty of tabernacle care, such that anyone else who approached it would be put to death.[1]

This reversal of fates is remarkable when we consider the extent to which Levi's legacy parallels that of Cain. Cain was the first killer. In slaughtering Abel, he established a trajectory of bloodshed that culminated in a world so full of violence that God purged it with a flood. Likewise, all that we know about the man Levi is that he violently killed many men, with the help of his brother. God declared Cain to be "cursed" from the ground and a fugitive and wanderer on the earth.[2] In the same way, Jacob curses the violence of his son Levi and declares that he will be scattered throughout Israel, with no tribal land to call his own.[3] Up until this point, their stories run remarkably parallel.

---

1. Cf. Num 18:6–7 and Num 1:51.
2. Gen 4:11–12.
3. Gen 49:5–7.

The next events in both accounts are also comparable, yet they feature contrasting outcomes. Cain fears that when people hear he killed someone, they will want to kill him. God addresses his concern by declaring that anyone who kills Cain will be avenged sevenfold. Cain then departs from God's presence and seeks refuge by building the first city.[4] Conversely, after Levi's descendants become priests, they maintain and guard the tabernacle of God's presence. The Levites, thus, draw nearer to God than everyone else. In addition, God places the Levites in charge of the cities of refuge to which those who kill people find protection, lest anyone strive to avenge the blood of the deceased prematurely. The connection of both stories to sacrifices also bears notice. Whereas Levi's descendants manage all sacrifices, Cain's failure to offer a pleasing sacrifice prompted his murder of Abel. In sum, although the man Levi left a legacy much like that of Cain, Levi's priestly descendants inherited responsibilities inversely proportional to that of Cain.

The event that moved God to exchange the Levites' ancestral curse for a blessing remains to be discussed. Exodus 32 records that event.[5] After Israel accepts God's covenant, Moses ascends the mountain to work out the details with God. Immediately the fledgling nation pressures Aaron to lead them in worshipping a golden calf. God was furious. In fact, Moses has to talk him out of destroying all other Israelites and starting over with him. After God relents, Moses summons all who were truly on God's side. Only the sons of Levi step forward. Moses then straps them with swords and sends them among the people to kill their own friends, family, and neighbors. Because they forsook such bonds and shed blood at God's behest, Moses says to them, "Today you have ordained yourselves for the service of the Lord, each one at the cost of a son or a brother, and so have brought a blessing on yourselves this day" (v. 29). The man Levi spurned the blood of strangers (the Shechemites) for the sake of family honor (Dinah); the sons of Levi now spurn familial blood to honor

---

4. Gen 4:13–17.

5. It is worth noting that Deuteronomy 33:8–11 identifies a different episode, the Israelites grumbling about water (cf. Exod 17:1–7 and Num 20:2–13), as the occasion of the Levite's reversal of fortune. For detailed analysis of this textual problem and a possible solution, see Joel S. Baden, "The Violent Origin of the Levites: Text and Tradition," in *Levites and Priests in Biblical History and Tradition*, eds. Mark Leuchter and Jeremy M. Hutton, 103–116 (Atlanta, GA: Society of Biblical Literature, 2011). Though the occasion and location differ, the reason for the reversal remains constant—placing devotion to God above kin—which is most important for my purposes.

God's exclusive claim on blood. This about-face constitutes their ordination into priestly service and everything that comes with it.

To serve God as priest requires honoring the sacredness of animal and human blood, the life their blood represents, and God's exclusive jurisdiction over lifeblood. God requires this perspective of those who oversee all divinely ordained sacrifices and who maintain the sanctuary where they are carried out. Having demonstrated this perspective, God authorizes specific Levites (Aaron's sons) to shed blood to atone for sin, complete goodwill offerings, and prepare animals for consumption. No one else may do so.[6] Crucially, however, God does not give these priests the "right" to take life. He only entrusts them with responsibility for carrying out his specific instructions as to how and when life may be taken. One single theme dominates the priestly instruction about sacrifices: they must be implemented exactly according to God's bidding.[7] Life is too important to improvise the shedding of blood.

The priests' role in warfare is also instructive. Though we commonly think of killing animals in sacrificial terms, Scripture speaks of killing humans in a similar way. That applies whether the loss of life entails killing an individual killer, killing one's enemies in war, or killing idolaters. Genesis 9:4–6, which we discussed in chapter 5, discusses killing killers in the context of killing animals and the sacredness of blood. This connection laid a foundation for the blood sacrifice laws in Torah. When someone kills another, he defiles the land with their blood. Atonement must be made, for which only the blood of the killer will do.[8] Scripture also describes Israel's vanquishing of towns in Canaan in terms of whole burnt offerings. God commanded that all people, animals, and spoils were to be destroyed. As whole burnt offerings were totally consumed in fire and not enjoyed as food, so these cities were to be completely burned up and not picked over for valuable spoils of war.[9] A similar fate befell Israelite families and towns that defiled the land with idolatry.[10]

Given the connection between killing humans and sacrifice, it is noteworthy that the Levites were *not* numbered among the fighting men whom

---

6. At first, God allowed only the priests to kill animals, even for ordinary consumption (Lev 17:1–7). But God later permitted other Israelites to do so for an ordinary meal but not a formal sacrifice (Deut 12:20–25). However, the people still needed to drain the blood properly from the animals before cooking and consuming them.

7. E.g., Lev 16.

8. Num 35:33.

9. Num 21:2; Deut 2:34; 3:6; 7:2; 20:17; and Josh 6:18.

10. Exod 22:20; Deut 13:12–18; and Josh 7:10–26.

God enlisted to "sacrifice" the Canaanites on his behalf.[11] Instead, the majority of them were responsible to care for the tabernacle. A select group of them were also called to remind the fighting men, by word and trumpet, that they were participating in God's war and not their own.[12] Moses explains,

> When you go out to war against your enemies, and see horses and chariots, an army larger than your own, you shall not be afraid of them; for the LORD your God is with you, who brought you up from the land of Egypt. Before you engage in battle, *the priest shall come forward and speak to the troops*, and shall say to them: "Hear, O Israel! Today you are drawing near to do battle against your enemies. Do not lose heart, or be afraid, or panic, or be in dread of them; for it is the LORD your God who goes with you, to fight for you against your enemies, to give you victory." (Deut 20:1–4)

As in the sacrificial system, the priests guarded God's exclusive jurisdiction over life, even in war. For war is truly a sacrificial act. No elder, king, or military commander makes the decision to go to war. God alone makes that decision. It is then relayed by priests who consult God by way of Urim, Ark, and Ephod.[13] Levites were, perhaps, ideal candidates for discerning God's will for war because they were not soldiers and they were not responsible for tribal lands and their borders. As perpetual exiles, they were less vested in the outcome of each war—having less to gain and less to lose. They were, thus, more likely to honor God's wishes.

This theme continues throughout the Old Testament in various ways. King Saul, for instance, lost his throne because he forsook God's exclusive claim on blood, as well as the priests' sacred duty to uphold it. In 1 Samuel 13, Saul grows impatient with the priest Samuel's delay. As a result, Saul dedicates to God his war against the Philistines by offering a sacrifice that only Samuel was authorized to submit. Later on, God commands Saul to sacrifice in war all of the Amalekites and their animals like a whole burnt offering. Instead, Saul spares certain lives of his choosing in order, so he claimed, to sacrifice them later.[14] Saul did not likely believe he was bamboozling God.

---

11. Num 1:47–54.
12. Num 10:9; 31:6; and Josh 6:4–16.
13. Cf. Num 27:21; Judg 20:27–28; and 1 Sam 30:7–8.
14. 1 Sam 15:2–3, 15, 21.

Rather, in monarchical fashion, he probably assumed that the office of priest belonged under royal jurisdiction. Saul did not realize that all humans—priests, kings, and otherwise—lack authority to give and take life. God reserves such authority for himself and those to whom he delegates it. Kings must obey God's decree. Samuel, the priest, sets this record straight with the rhetorical question, "Has the LORD as great delight in burnt offerings and sacrifices, as in obeying the voice of the LORD?"[15] He then dispatches Saul as king and anoints David to succeed him. David follows Saul's bad example when he uses warfare to cover his own adultery and later takes a census of his fighting men (an act of preparation for war) without consulting a priest.[16] His repeated usurpation of priestly functions also spelled the end of his effective reign as king.[17]

Sacrifices played an important role in Israel's life together. Priests served as stewards of the entire system that governed them.[18] God knew that his people were disobedient and incapable of living a pure life. So he commissioned them to offer pure animals to stand in for the life they should be living and to remind them perpetually to renew their commitment to God's will for their life. Yet the priests and people could not live up to the obedience required for true sacrifice. Surrendering the best of their flocks did not elicit the best of their lives, so God intervened decisively. He offered up his best—his only Son Jesus—to be and to offer the true obedience and true sacrifice that God's people could not offer.[19] Jesus was the "end" of sacrifice in the sense of both fulfillment and termination. His death fulfills the ultimate purpose that the sacrificial system first served. As such, it strictly forbids and, therefore, terminates all future bloodletting in order to atone for sin.[20]

---

15. 1 Sam 15:22.

16. 2 Sam 11 and 24. Note, the priests Aaron and Eleazar were present during the first two censuses of the Israelites before waging war on Canaan (Num 1:4 and 26:1–4, 63–64).

17. Earlier on, David routinely inquired of the Lord before waging war (1 Sam 22:10; 23:2–4; 30:8; 2 Sam 2:1; and 5:19, 23). Although in 1 Samuel 30:7–8 he asserts his independence by getting an Ephod from the priest so he can inquire on his own.

18. For a helpful summary of the logic behind various sacrifices, see Nelson, *Raising Up a Faithful Priest*, 55–59.

19. Rom 3:23; Eph 5:2; Heb 9:26; 10:12; 1 John 2:2; and 4:10.

20. Heb 9:26–28. I discuss this theme at length in John C. Nugent, "End of Sacrifice: John Howard Yoder's Critique of Capital Punishment," in *Let Us Attend: The Theological Reading of Scripture as Political Act* (Minneapolis: Fortress Press, 2015), ch. 13.

RELATING TO GOD AND WORLD

The Jerusalem temple, which became the only legitimate place to offer sacrifices from Solomon's time forward, was providentially built on Mount Moriah.[21] This location proved providential because of the site's connection to the test of true obedience that undergirded Israelite faith. God asked Abraham to sacrifice Isaac, the child of promise, in that region.[22] Abraham's faith is evident not only in his trusting God with the life of his son, but also in his trusting God to provide the sacrifice.[23] Because God did so, the Israelites remembered that place as "Yahweh Yirah," the place where God provides.[24]

When it comes to sacrifice, God is always the one who provides. When it came to the sacrificial system, God provided animals to stand in for the lives that humans could not live. When it came to the social and cosmic order that was violated when humans or animals took the life of another, God provided that the life of the life-takers alone would atone to set things right. When it came to saving the Israelites from divine abandonment following covenant-breaking idolatry in their midst, God provided that the life of the offending household or tribe would stand in for the nation. When it came to saving a world bent on self-destruction and a chosen nation that forsook the role for which God chose it, God provided his Son to stand in for their collective disobedience. God alone can provide for sacrifice because no one else is capable of rendering what is required. This does not negate the human responsibility for selecting the best of their flocks and crops but, properly speaking, these offerings already belong to God.[25] Humans may only offer back what God already owns because God has provided that such offerings will count to him as that which humans are incapable of providing on their own.

Whether believers or unbelievers, all that humans can do is receive God's sacrifice as a gift. Though the gift God has provided cannot be earned, all humans will be held accountable for it. Should they reject God's gift and take their lives or that of others into their own hands, they will certainly be judged.[26] This prospect will not keep the Sauls of this world from taking life into

---

21. 2 Chron 3:1.
22. Gen 22:2.
23. Gen 22:8. This place is popularly translated as "Jehovah Jirah."
24. Gen 22:14.
25. Ps 89:11.
26. Matt 26:52 and Heb 10:26–31.

their own hands and justifying themselves with pious- and noble-sounding reasons. Yet in spurning God's sacrifice with all of its implications they, like the church addressed in the book of Hebrews, invite God's vengeance: "It is a fearful thing to fall into the hands of the living God" (Heb 10:29–31).

The unique role of God's people in relation to sacrifice and the wider world remains modest but critical: we are stewards of Christ's sacrifice and all that it means. We proclaim to everyone the good news of his victory over sin and death on the cross. We announce that God in Christ has strictly forbidden all further bloodletting to atone for sin—whether by ordained priests or civil magistrates. We stubbornly affirm God's exclusive claim on life in all spheres of creaturely existence. On behalf of the world and in the sight of all, we offer our own lives as living sacrifices by ordering them both individually and collectively according to God's sovereign will.[27]

IMPLICATIONS FOR THE CHURCH

When Christians think of Old Testament priests, they often think of sacrifices. When Christians think about sacrifices, they quickly jump to Jesus's once-for-all death on the cross to atone for sins and make us right with God. We thus tend to reduce priests and sacrifices to their vertical-spiritual significance. Consequently, Christians today overlook priesthood as a governing image for the church, especially in its relationship to the world. We've done so in recent decades to compensate for our past tendency to neglect the gospel's horizontal-social significance. As a result, the priestly image did not seem as useful as others.

I have no desire to downplay the vertical-spiritual dimensions of sacrifice and our priestly vocation. Those are critical, indeed essential to our salvation. Without them, we are lost. In this book, I argue that we need not leave the priestly image behind to recover the social dimensions of the gospel and the church's mission. To do so, I have been emphasizing the oft-neglected social dimensions of Israel's priests and their implications for the church. In keeping with that emphasis, this chapter highlights several oft-neglected social-political dimensions of Christ's sacrifice. If I were writing a complete treatise on the nature and implications of the cross, I would have to dedicate

---

27. Rom 12:1–2, Phil 2:12–18; and 1 Pet 2:4–12.

far more space to the vertical and internal-personal dimensions, but that important task lies beyond the scope of this book.[28]

Churches are not places where blood sacrifices are constantly made. Rather, they are communities among whom God's sacrifice to end all sacrifices remains central to our essence, ethic, and witness to the world. Our stewardship of Christ's sacrifice has numerous practical implications for church life. Here I discuss five.

Honor Life with Our Lives

The Old Testament makes quite clear that blood is sacred because life is in the blood.[29] Consequently, blood plays a significant role in the sacrificial system. And blood offenses, like murder, require utter seriousness. The New Testament also takes blood quite seriously. When the Jerusalem council, recorded in Acts, composed a letter that identifies which laws from the old covenant are still binding on the new covenant community, two of them focused specifically on blood.[30] The letter reads as follows:

> For it has seemed good to the Holy Spirit and to us to impose on you no further burden than these essentials: that you abstain from what has been sacrificed to idols and from blood and from what is strangled and from fornication. If you keep yourselves from these, you will do well. Farewell. (Acts 15:28–29)

God forbids eating "strangled" meat because strangled animals are cooked with their blood still in them. That leads to consuming blood. Since life is in the blood, such consumption is outlawed in Torah.[31] The council uses only the word "blood" to identify another forbidden practice. The Greek might better be translated "bloodguilt." This differs from strangled animals because it represents a broader category that represents violating the sanctity of human

---

28. For a more complete assessment of the sacrificial system and the meaning of Christ's death, see episodes 3.25–43 of the After Class Podcast, which I cohost with two colleagues, Ron Peters and Sam Long. https://afterclass.libsyn.com.

29. For a detailed examination of blood in the Bible, see William K. Gilders, *Blood Ritual in the Hebrew Bible* (Baltimore & London: Johns Hopkins University Press, 2004).

30. Arguably, all four have to do with blood, since fornication violates the sanctity of marriage, which is a blood covenant, and idolatry violates our blood covenant with God.

31. Lev 17:10–14.

life. One incurs bloodguilt by violating human life. As a result, the victim's blood is upon them. The offense must be atoned for by shedding the offender's blood. Murder stands as the most obvious blood offense, but others include offering illicit sacrifices, cursing parents, sacrificing children, practicing sexual aberrations, and becoming mediums or wizards.[32]

The Jerusalem council is not suggesting that people who commit such offenses be killed, but that Gentile converts to Christianity should abstain from such practices. In so doing, the council affirms that blood remains sacred to believers and that they should do everything in their power to honor the sanctity of life. That Jesus took on flesh and blood, forbade all acts of violence, gave his own life as the sacrifice to end all sacrifices, and died not just for good people but for all people reinforced and strengthened his followers' commitment to the sanctity of life.

As stewards of Christ's sacrifice, today's church must continue to honor the sanctity of life in every aspect of our lives. We can do so in many ways, but I submit the following practices to get the conversation started:

- Carry babies to full term, even when they appear to be unhealthy or nonviable. Support pregnant women who struggle to keep their babies for any reason by tending to their emotional, physical, and financial needs. Offer to adopt and raise unwanted children of any age.
- Ascribe value to lives that society deems worthless, whether due to age, loss of mobility, cognitive impairment, criminal activity, or public enemy status.
- Accept the finality of death and resist the urge to summon or otherwise bring back a life that God has allowed to die. The deceased belong to God and their eternal state rests in his hands. All forms of necromancy remain off limits.
- Love our enemies—whether personal, societal, or national—by rejecting the temptation to enact vengeance upon them and by refusing to take their lives under any circumstance. Nothing they

---

32. For murder, see Deut 19:11–12 and 21:8; for unauthorized sacrifices, see Lev 17:3–4; for child sacrifice, see Lev 20:1–5; for cursing one's parents, see Lev 20:9; for sexually aberrant behavior, see Lev 20:11–13, 16; for becoming wizards or mediums, see Lev 20:27.

might take from us or from those we love is worth usurping God's exclusive claim on their lives.

- Reject the practice of creating life. Making extensive use of science to heal a person, restore their bodies, and keep them alive (within limits) differs from playing God by striving to create or engineer new life.

- Pursue careers that uphold, protect, and perpetuate the sanctity of life and avoid those that take life, degrade life, or profit from those who do.

- Avoid forms of entertainment that make sport of taking life or otherwise degrading it. This may be difficult given the pervasiveness of violence in contemporary media, but believers should at least commit to avoiding the most gratuitously violent books, shows, and games. Starting there would show great progress.

- Pray and advocate for those whose lives are at risk, including but not limited to inmates on death row, soldiers at war, peacemakers on the front lines, Christians in areas rife with persecution, and those who have no one to safeguard the sanctity of their life.

- Value and care for the lives of animals. We may do this in a variety of ways, including how we eat, dress, hunt, shop, raise our pets, treat wild animals, and care for the environments in which they live. Animals possess the same lifeblood as humans. The way one treats animal life is often connected to how one treats humans whose lives are deemed less valuable. I return to this later in the chapter.

Lay Down Our Lives

Though a child of the eighties, I began taking my faith seriously in the 1990s. At that time, the phrase "What Would Jesus Do?" made a huge resurgence in the United States, sparked in part by the proliferation of WWJD bracelets.[33] We all shared a sense that Jesus would want us to live moral lives and be radically loving to other people, especially those in need and those who seemed

---

33. As well as the publication of Garrett W. Sheldon, *What Would Jesus Do?* (Nashville, TN: Broadman & Holman Pub, 1998), a retelling of his grandfather's classic, Charles Sheldon, *In His Steps: "What Would Jesus Do?"* (Chicago: Advance Publishing, 1898).

difficult to love. The concept hooked me. So as I advanced in my ministerial and theological training, I eventually followed this train of thought to its logical conclusions: loving my enemies to the point of death. For the first time, I took the Christian peace witness seriously. I must really be willing to lay down my life.

Irrelevant Jesus[34]

Not everyone agrees. An influential thinker at a theological conference shocked me when he pejoratively dismissed the Christian peace witness. He provided simple reasoning: Jesus didn't come to show us how to live or even teach us how to live. Instead, he came to die for our sins so we could be saved. How Jesus lived and what he taught is "incidental" to Jesus's mission and to ours. This theologian concluded that making much of Jesus's lifestyle or teachings for Christian ethics was, therefore, theologically erroneous. I wasn't shocked that someone would actually believe this, since many scholars don't take Jesus or the Bible all that seriously. I was shocked because the person who affirmed this was an influential conservative known for his high view of Scripture.

This raised the question with greater urgency, Did Jesus actually set an example that he expected his disciples to follow until his return? My reading confirmed that others supported this man's claims. Different scholars reject the relevance of Jesus's example for a variety of reasons:

- Jesus thought the world would end soon, but he was wrong.
- Jesus's ways were only for the disciples who followed him around Palestine.
- Jesus provided a model for our private lives and church families only.
- Jesus offered a preview of the age to come and not a blueprint for life in this age.
- Jesus set forth an impossible ideal so we would be overwhelmed by our inability to keep it and consequently throw ourselves upon his mercy and grace.

---

34. This section heading is inspired by Gerhard Lohfink's provocative book, *No Irrelevant Jesus: On Jesus and the Church Today*, translated by Linda M. Maloney (Collegeville, MN: Liturgical Press, 2014).

I needed to cross-examine these claims with those of Scripture. So I began a meticulous study of the New Testament. I focused on how Jesus framed his most difficult teachings and observed how various Apostolic letters interacted with his lived example. I also consulted influential scholars who had taken up the same task.[35] I concluded that the New Testament does, in fact, regard Jesus's life and teachings as the standard for all believers in all times and places. For the kingdom Jesus brought has already begun and the church's mission entails embracing, displaying, and proclaiming that kingdom to the wider world. God gives us his Spirit precisely because Christians cannot complete this task by our own strength. The first-century church didn't expect that the unbelieving world would or could follow the way of Jesus—not without God's empowering presence and certainly not without faith.[36] The New Testament Scriptures do not evaluate the way of Jesus according to its efficacy in running the current world but by its fidelity in welcoming the world to come.

Doing What Christ Did

Numerous New Testament passages call believers to imitate the life of Jesus, but not in every aspect.[37] They do not call us to imitate his maleness, divinity, ability to calm storms, or skill as a tradesman. Rather, they call us to appropriate *his stance toward people* through humble serving, costly loving, and generous giving. They call us to follow *his approach to adversity* by loving our enemies, forgiving those who have wronged us, and enduring suffering with joy. They call us to embrace *his triumph over sin* by dying to our old sinful ways and pursuing new life in the Spirit in holiness and purity. By a wide margin, the three most cited ways the New Testament calls us to imitate Jesus include his humble serving, costly loving, and joyful suffering. Each of these ways entails laying down our lives in one way or another.

---

35. A landmark work in the regard, numbered among *Christianity Today*'s top ten most influential Christian books of the twentieth century, is John H. Yoder's *The Politics of Jesus: Vicit Agnus Noster*, 2nd ed. (Grand Rapids, MI: Eerdmans, 1994).

36. 1 Cor 2:6–14 and Heb 11:6.

37. Matt 5:43–48; 18:32–33; 20:25–28; Mark 10:42–45; Luke 6:32–36; John 13:14–15; 13:34; 15:12; 15:20–21; Rom 6:6–11; 8:29; 13:14; 15:1–3; 15:7; 1 Cor 10:31–11:1; 2 Cor 1:5; 3:18; 4:8–11; 8:7–9; Eph 4:17–24; 4:32; 5:1–2; 5:25; Phil 2:5–8; 3:10–11; Col 1:24; 2:6 (cf. 3:9–17); 1 Thess 1:6; 1 Pet 1:15–16; 2:20–25; 3:14–18; 4:1–2; 4:12–16; 1 John 1:5–7; 2:3–11; 3:1–3; 3:11–16; and 4:7–21.

Self-Sacrifice

As stewards of Christ's sacrifice, we must be willing to lay down our lives. We must take up our cross and follow him, even when that means suffering for our faith at the hands of our enemies. We point others to Jesus not just by talking about his sacrifice but by living it out in our bodies. As Paul puts it, "present your bodies as a living sacrifice, holy and acceptable to God, which is your spiritual worship" (Rom 12:1).

A New Testament professor of mine, Rollin Ramsaran, clarified that nature of Christian sacrifice in a way that stuck with me.[38] He said that Christian sacrifice is not *self-sacrifice*, defined as the negation of ourselves, but *self-giving*, which entails giving of ourselves on behalf of others. He put this in algebraic terms. Where S stands for self, self-sacrifice amounts to $S - S = 0$.[39] When we sacrifice ourselves, we end up with nothing. But that's not what happened with Jesus and not what he asks of us. When Christ emptied himself, became a servant, and gave up his life for the world, he gained a glorified resurrection body and exaltation to God's right hand with all powers and principalities subject to him. When we die to ourselves by pouring our lives out for others, we also stand to gain. Jesus promised his followers, "there is no one who has left house or brothers or sisters or mother or father or children or fields, for my sake and for the sake of the good news, who will not receive a hundredfold now in this age—houses, brothers and sisters, mothers and children, and fields with persecutions—and in the age to come eternal life" (Mark 10:29–30). In the kingdom calculus of self-giving, $S - S = 100S + \infty$.[40] Or, in Paul's words, "to me, living is Christ and dying is gain" (Phil 1:21).

Joyful Sacrifice

We often miss this dimension of sacrifice because we tend to view sacrifices as whole burnt offerings, the kind where fire consumes the entire offering.[41] Understandably so, since the book of Leviticus begins with whole burnt

---

38. Though I have adapted his thought somewhat, I am indebted to Dr. Ramsaran for this basic idea.

39. For the mathematically challenged: Self minus Self equals Zero, kind of like 2-2=0.

40. This time, Self minus Self equals one hundred times Self plus Infinity, kind of like 2-2=200 + ∞. This, of course, is mathematical nonsense, which is why the wisdom of the cross is foolishness to those who reject it (1 Cor 1:18).

41. E.g., Lev 1:1–17.

offerings and people often start skimming after that. But not all offerings were completely consumed. Many were celebratory. People would bring their animals to be slaughtered. The inedible parts would be burned and a portion of the meat would be shared with the priests. Then the one who brought the offering would feast on what remained with his guests. They would also offer up grain and wine because meat goes best with bread and something to drink. They participated in such offerings to celebrate a special occasion—a reason for feasting and joy. So when we seek first God's kingdom by placing others before ourselves at the cost of our own time, money, and prestige, we reap a harvest of abundant life in Christ, in whom "it is more blessed to give than receive" (Acts 20:35).

Yet this does not mean we will always enjoy giving of ourselves sacrificially for the kingdom. We are encouraged to endure pain, suffering, abuse, hostility, afflictions, persecutions, struggles, and scorn precisely because laying down our lives often hurts.[42] The ultimate suffering leads to death. Even in the face of death, we are called to be witnesses. The Greek word for witness became the English word for martyr.[43] There is no greater way to steward Christ's sacrifice than to face death for his name's sake. In so doing, we bear witness to what Jesus did on behalf of this world and to our unflinching hope in his eternal kingdom.

Proclaim Christ's Jurisdiction Over Life

Jesus is Lord. That seems like a simple enough statement, perhaps even a relatively harmless one. In popular use, one might say it to identify as a Christian. It's a way of saying that one belongs to the religion of Jesus, as opposed to Moses, Mohammed, Buddha, or Mary Baker Eddy. For the early church, however, to proclaim Jesus as Lord constituted a bold declaration—not just a claim about religious affiliation, but a claim about the universe.

From the very beginning, the early church proclaimed Jesus as Lord of all, seated at God's right hand.[44] When Jesus ascended into heaven,

---

42. E.g., 1 Cor 4:12; 2 Cor 1:6; 2 Thess 1:4; 2 Tim 2:5; Heb 10:32; 12:3, 7; 13:13; and 1 Pet 2:19.

43. The connection between witnesses and death is evident in Acts 22:20; Rev 1:5; 2:13; and 17:6.

44. Acts 2:32–36; 10:36; and Phil 2:9–11.

they recognized him as much more than a religious leader for Jews in Palestine. Rather, he is Lord over all people and indeed all creation. In an early Christian hymn, they sang "at the name of Jesus every knee should bend, in heaven and on earth and under the earth, and every tongue should confess that Jesus Christ is Lord" (Phil 2:10–11). This kind of talk upset political leaders, like Caesar, who saw themselves as lords and saviors of the known world and proclaimed as much on their coinage and royal insignias.

But perhaps this scandalous "Jesus talk" amounted only to lofty rhetoric. Were these Christians simply saying that Jesus is Lord over all of those who choose to bend the knee and confess him as such? Not according to the apostle Paul. He makes clear that their vision was much grander than that:

> He is the image of the invisible God, the firstborn of all creation; for in him all things in heaven and on earth were created, things visible and invisible, whether thrones or dominions or rulers or powers—all things have been created through him and for him. He himself is before all things, and in him all things hold together. (Col 1:15–17)

The lordship of Christ means that all rulers and powers have come into being through him and continue to exist only to serve his purposes. *He* is the one who glues this world together, not the world's hallowed legal systems or complex web of emperors, governors, and prefects.

Or maybe the cry "Jesus is Lord" is best interpreted as a statement of faith about the future. Sure, God has raised Jesus. But Jesus doesn't really control things yet. Christians were a persecuted minority, and Roman authorities clearly managed the nations. When Christ returns to set things right, he will assume control. But, for now, the governing authorities rule. Again this vision falls short of the early church's confession. Paul elsewhere explains that God exalted Christ "far above all rule and authority and power and dominion, and above every name that is named, *not only in this age* but also in the age to come" (Eph 1:21). The order of that last phrase means we cannot reduce Christ's reign to an entirely futuristic hope. Paul took for granted that Christ was exalted over all rulers "in this age." He emphasizes, instead, that Christ's reign would not stop when this age ends. After God consummates his ultimate purposes for all creation, Christ will *still* be Lord of all!

Christ above All Things

You may be wondering how all this lordship talk pertains to our priestly stewardship of Christ's sacrifice. For Paul, Christ's lordship and priestly stewardship have everything to do with one another. Consider how he finishes the above quote from Colossians:

> He is the head of the body, the church; he is the beginning, the firstborn from the dead, so that he might come to have first place in everything. For in him all the fullness of God was pleased to dwell, and through him God was pleased to reconcile to himself all things, whether on earth or in heaven, by making peace through the blood of his cross. (Col 1:18–20)

The pressing agenda of the exalted Lord is to lead his church. He first instructed them to confess him as "first in all things." They must proclaim and embody the new reality that Christ has reconciled all things to himself and made peace through his sacrifice on the cross. This echoes Paul's statement to the Corinthians, which further specifies the church's role:

> If anyone is in Christ, there is a new creation: everything old has passed away; see, everything has become new! All this is from God, who reconciled us to himself through Christ, and has given us the ministry of reconciliation; that is, in Christ God was reconciling the world to himself, not counting their trespasses against them, and entrusting the message of reconciliation to us. So we are ambassadors for Christ, since God is making his appeal through us. (2 Cor 5:17–20)

The body of Christ forms the "new creation" community. We have accepted Christ's gift of reconciliation and entered into the newness of life. But God is not content to stop with us. He was reconciling the whole world to himself in Christ and the world doesn't even realize that he no longer holds their sins against them. Since they need to be told, he appointed us as ambassadors. We live as citizens of the new creation who represent God's gift of forgiveness and reconciliation on alien turf to those still beholden to the old order that is passing away.

In the Old Testament, God affirms the sanctity of all life by pointing to the lifeblood we all share in common. In a world reeling from escalating vengeance, God uses the "life for life" principle to keep violence in check. To cleanse the land of bloodguilt, he commanded his people to sacrifice only the life of the killer. Such rules were directionally redemptive. They took a bad situation and made it better. But violence didn't stop there and neither did God. Through Christ's sacrifice, he atoned for sin "once and for all."[45] All people sin and fall short of God's glory, but Christ gifts us with eternal life. The woman caught in adultery deserved to be stoned, but Jesus sent the rock peddlers packing. Those who killed an innocent man at the behest of an unruly mob, deserved to die. But Christ prayed, "Father, forgive them; for they do not know what they are doing" (Luke 23:34).

Again, this wasn't just Jesus being Jesus, as if he said this only because he had to die on the cross to save us all from sin. While an angry mob was stoning Stephen, a second-generation disciple, he prayed the same prayer.[46] Christ doesn't want killers to die. Their lives remain sacred to him. He came so they might truly live. He went so far as to take Saul, the Christian killer who orchestrated the murder of Stephen, and use him to kickstart the church's mission to the nations. What great news! If Saul's life remained sacred, if even he could be saved, then so can today's worst sinners. And how will they know unless we tell them?[47]

Playing God

We live in a time when people in power think they have the right to give and take life. They believe that climbing the ranks and securing the favor of the right people entitles them to use their power to determine who gets to live and die. A surprising number of people routinely make these kinds of decisions, including politicians, lawmakers, juries, military officers, policemen, executioners, assassins, security guards, doctors, and scientists. In all such cases, some individual or group decides the criteria by which certain people are deemed worthy of death.

A friend of mine had a brother who needed heart surgery. When I first began writing this chapter, his life hung in the balance. Doctors didn't know when his heart would give out, but they knew it would be soon. A few days before his scheduled surgery, my friend's brother, who suffered

---

45. Cf. Heb 7:27; 9:12, 26; and 10:10.
46. Acts 7:60.
47. Rom 10:14–15.

from drug addiction, got cold feet. To everyone's dismay, he checked himself out of the hospital and went somewhere to get high. His body declined quickly, so he returned to the hospital. Upon his return, the doctor canceled the surgery indefinitely. This surgeon deemed a flight risk drug addict unworthy of a new heart and deserving of a preventable death. He died within a month.

People of power will kill for a variety of reasons. Some of the most common offenses include trespassing private property, posing a threat, siding with the enemy, trafficking drugs, committing treason, attempting to kill someone, or engaging in egregious acts of violence. Executioners cope with blood on their hands by reminding themselves that they are just doing their jobs. They don't decide who lives or dies; they merely carry out the judgment of others.

Unauthorized Slaying

But if you believe, as a matter of faith and obedience to Scripture, that Christ is Lord over every authority, then such justification falls short. Christ has nowhere authorized the taking of life. In Romans, Paul teaches that God will repay everyone for what they have done on the day of wrath when the secret thoughts of human hearts are revealed.[48] Consistent with that, he later instructs believers not to avenge themselves but to leave room for God's wrath.[49] So far, it seems like Paul is upholding the Old Testament teaching that decisions about life and death belong to God alone.

Paul then encourages the Roman church to live on good terms with sword-bearing governing authorities because God uses them as his servants to encourage good conduct and execute wrath on bad conduct.[50] To some, the fact that God uses *sword-bearing* authorities to motivate good civil conduct means God has authorized them to kill people as they see fit.[51] While possible, this interpretation strains credulity. In the first century, swords were used to kill, but more often they served as symbols of authority to intimidate and

---

48. Rom 2:5–16.
49. Rom 12:19.
50. Rom 13:1–4.
51. It would have to be "as they see fit" because God nowhere gives guidelines to Roman authorities or anyone else as to when they may kill someone.

deter unlawful behavior.[52] They also served as multipurpose tools for a variety of reasons, including self-defense and wounding but not killing someone.[53] Peter offers a parallel account of the authorities' role. In his view, they serve "to punish those who do wrong and to praise those who do right" (1 Pet 2:14). Paul likely had these same two functions in mind. Positively, the authorities reward; negatively they punish—not kill.

This interpretation aligns well with Paul's testimony and teachings. Consider, for example, his words to Timothy:

> I am grateful to Christ Jesus our Lord, who has strengthened me, because he judged me faithful and appointed me to his service, even though I was formerly a blasphemer, a persecutor, and a man of violence. But I received mercy because I had acted ignorantly in unbelief, and the grace of our Lord overflowed for me with the faith and love that are in Christ Jesus. The saying is sure and worthy of full acceptance, that Christ Jesus came into the world to save sinners—of whom I am the foremost. But for that very reason I received mercy, so that in me, as the foremost, Jesus Christ might display the utmost patience, making me an example to those who would come to believe in him for eternal life. (1 Tim 1:12–16)

Though Paul lived a life of violence, indeed murder, God showed him mercy and grace. He sinned worse than anyone else. Yet, the exalted Christ dealt patiently with him, consistent with his mission to save sinners. Paul thus serves as an example for egregious sinners who may also receive mercy, grace, and eternal life. It stretches the imagination to think that the man who wrote this to Timothy elsewhere provides the only New Testament justification for humans killing other humans at their own discretion. The authoritative status of certain humans doesn't significantly change things. Before his conversion, Paul solicited permission from authorities to legitimate his own pogrom against Christians, which surely wasn't right.[54] He also acted quite obstinately when Roman authorities overstepped their jurisdiction and mistreated a Roman citizen.[55] He certainly wouldn't have written them a blank check to kill.

---

52. E.g., Luke 22:52.
53. E.g., Luke 22:36, 49 and Mark 14:47.
54. Acts 9:1–2.
55. Acts 16:37.

Christian Proclamation

As priestly stewards of Christ's sacrifice, Christians should proclaim Christ's lordship over all life. We must condemn all acts of bloodshed, even ones committed under the guise of proper authority. Where, when, and how to accomplish this presents a challenge. One thing is certain: we must react to bloodshed as exiles commissioned to proclaim Christ's sacrifice as God's gift to the world. This framing means everything. The lordship of Christ over all authorities serves as the basis of our proclamation to world powers. We act as ambassadors in exile. Our proclamation should center on Christ's sacrifice to end all sacrifices.

Possible occasions for such proclamation include pulpits, publications, parenting, polls, and protests. Our unique posture and commission mean that we will not behave on such occasions the ways unbelievers do. Joining protests alongside unbelievers may drown out our specific message or confuse it with a non-redemptive worldly one. We may want to stage our own protest. Voting also poses unique challenges. Elections often threaten to suck us into a worldly platform or narrative with false choices framed by partisan politics. We may prefer local elections and opportunities to vote on specific issues rather than broad party-line packages. I return to the subject of public proclamation in chapter 8.

Appreciate Lives that Make Ours Possible

The Old Testament doles out harsh punishments to rebellious children, which comes as a surprise to many readers. It creates a violent perception of the Israelites and their God for some people. Our fondness for laws that forbid sacrificing children to foreign gods is chastened by those that sanction stoning children for bad behavior.[56] Grounds for execution include striking parents, cursing parents, and sloughing off parental discipline to live lives of gluttony and drunkenness.[57]

It is tempting to see Israelite faith as harsh and controlling. It is easy to read Scripture backwards. We compare ancient times to our own day, rather than reading the text forward to see how it speaks in the context when the author wrote it. A contextual reading suggests that these strict laws were grounded

---

56. For child sacrifice, see Lev 18:21.
57. Exod 21:15, 17; Lev 20:9; and Deut 21:18–21.

less in a low view of children and more in a high view of parenting. God recognized the pivotal role parents play in raising up the next generation of Israelites capable of continuing his mission.[58] Consequently, honoring parents is a prerequisite for living long in the land of promise.[59] Modern translations can also skew our reading of these texts. The term "children" evokes images of young and vulnerable dependents, usually from birth to adolescence. Newer translations often use this term as a gender-neutral substitute for "sons." The term could just as easily refer to young people or adults. Clamping down on abuse of older, vulnerable parents by their adult children differs entirely from coming down hard on younglings struggling to find their way.

Be that as it may, respect for parents is grounded in respect for life itself. Consider Leviticus 20:9, "All who curse father or mother shall be put to death; having cursed father or mother, their blood is upon them." The phrase "their blood is upon them" suggests that cursing parents was a bloodguilt offense. Such offenses demanded the taking of life because they transgressed the sacred bounds of life. Bloodguilt offenses usually involved deliberately taking a life, violating the marital act of reproduction, or meddling with the realm of the dead. As such, laws proscribing blatant disregard for one's parents served to remind the Israelites that they received life as a gift, and that all Israelites must honor those through whom God gave them life.

Of course, I am not suggesting that Christians today revive the ancient practice of stoning rebellious offspring. Rather, these laws convey a deep respect and appreciation for those who have made our lives possible. Stewards of Christ's sacrifice should be no less respectful and appreciative. Since Christ's death is God's ultimate affirmation of life's sacredness, Christians should stand out for their deep appreciation for all who make their lives possible. This can take several forms. Here I discuss four of them.

Honoring Parents

In a culture that prizes freedom and independence above all, stewards of Christ's sacrifice should honor their parents. Without them we don't exist, yet leaving them behind is easy. In a highly mobile and independent culture, we seldom live close to them. So the maxim prevails, "out of sight, out of mind."

---

58. Gen 18:19; Deut 4:9–10; 6:1–2; and 11:18–19.
59. Exod 20:12.

As parents age, the wider citizenry tends to see them as less productive, less in touch, and less useful. They've stopped contributing fiscally and now mostly drain funds and resources from the societal collective.

The aged regularly find themselves ignored or neglected by those around them, which only gets worse when a spouse dies and leaves them without a consistent advocate. Christ may call his followers to leave their parents to pursue kingdom mission, but he sends no one out to pursue the American dream. One who fails to provide for family, according to 1 Timothy 5:8, "has denied the faith and is worse than an unbeliever." Jesus himself cared for his mother and provided for her care after his departure.[60]

Christians can, therefore, shine brightly by showing uncommon appreciation and concern for their parents. We do so not just by making sure their basic needs are covered; most unbelievers do that. Rather, because Christ esteems their lives as precious, we care for them in ways that uphold their dignity and demonstrate our appreciation for the gift of life they have given us. We want them to thrive, not merely survive. In addition, since many children cannot or do not ensure the thriving of their parents, churches can step in and help. Together, we can provide the familial respect and appreciation that the aging in our midst fail to receive from their own children. In so doing, we honor the sanctity of life from womb to tomb.

Honoring Workers

Our lives also depend on the tireless work of countless people who devote the majority of their waking hours to providing our food and resources, whether on farms or in factories. Stewards of Christ's sacrifice, therefore, honor the workers who provide our daily bread. Most workers render their service in the shadows. The fruit of their labor simply appears on store shelves, if not in bags or boxes on our front porches. Genesis 3 makes clear that these products don't come easily. Cursed soil requires hours of tedious or strenuous labor, sometimes in harsh conditions that can suck the life from people. Our society simply presumes such service.

Stewards of Christ's sacrifice express uncommon appreciation for the toil of others. We do so by lifting them up in prayer each time we eat or otherwise benefit from the fruit of their labor. We do so by willingly paying taxes and

---

60. John 19:26–27.

insurance that compensates for shortfalls they experience due to droughts or natural disasters that undercut their livelihood. When they belong to our community, we share in the work, offer assistance when needed, and do what we can to ensure they receive needed rest on a regular basis. As far as it depends on us, we advocate for working conditions befitting those made in God's image and help shoulder the burden when current conditions fall short.

Honoring Non-Human Creation

Knowing that Christ is Lord over all creation and all things were created in him and for him means that stewards of his sacrifice will also honor non-human creation. Here I am thinking of land and seas, plant and animal life. They all comprise God's good gift to humanity. They all groan under the curse of sin. And they will all experience Christ's restoration of all things.[61]

We must be careful not to reduce mealtime prayers to empty rituals. When Jesus broke bread, he routinely gave thanks. I suspect he truly meant it. Forty days of fasting certainly put him in touch with his body's dependence on food. Few North American Christians today go far enough between meals to feel the actual pain of deprivation. The early Christians called their meals Eucharists, which means thanksgiving. When they broke bread, they thanked God for Jesus and for providing their sustenance. We should do the same, with all sincerity.

Animals deserve special attention, since God gave them such in Scripture. The same lifeblood that flows in us flows in them. Their lives, too, are sacred. When their lives are taken so we may eat a meal, the act remains a real sacrifice. Their blood must still be properly drained, and we should thank God for them before consuming their flesh. As stewards of Christ's sacrifice, believers should also honor the sacredness of animal life in how we herd and hunt. If we are going to eat animals, we should exemplify humane treatment of them while they live under our care. Their meat isn't like fruit that one plucks from a tree. The tree lives on to produce again and again.

For us to eat meat, some creature must stop living, permanently. In anticipation of God's kingdom, some choose to abstain from meat altogether.[62]

---

61. Acts 3:21 and Rom 8:18–22.
62. Cf. Stephen H. Webb, *Good Eating*, The Christian Practice of Everyday Life (Grand Rapids: Brazos, 2001).

Christ does not require vegetarianism, but we might consider it. Like celibacy, this practice can provide a faithful pointer and reminder of God's kingdom. When exposed to a vegetarian lifestyle on a regular basis, those who choose to consume meat will be less likely to take for granted and dishonor the life offered on their behalf.

Remember Christ's Sacrifice of His Own Life

Fifth, and finally, priestly stewards must continually remember Christ's sacrifice for the world. In some ways, the remembrance of Christ's sacrifice creates the center from which the above four practices follow. Without it we compromise our priestly stewardship. *Our reverence for life* devolves into secular humanism. Like the world, we begin honoring lives that society happens to honor. *Laying down our lives* devolves into personal heroism or some sort of savior complex. Those who draw excessive attention to themselves take their admirers down with them when they eventually fall. *Our proclamation of Christ's jurisdiction over all life* devolves into an ideological shouting match. We must take care that our voice is not assimilated into whichever political lobbying group appears most like us. *Our appreciation for the lives that make ours possible* devolves into obligation or tokenism. We might resort to the bare minimum, which only adds disgrace to those we seek to honor.

We need Christ's sacrifice to remind us that our priestly stewardship exemplifies God's love for the whole world. We receive God's gift of a restored and reconciled world according to God's perfect will for the full flourishing of all creation. The following four practices keep the sacrifice of Christ at the forefront of our minds.

Breaking Bread

We remember Christ's sacrifice first and foremost by breaking bread together. Christ has given us this meal to remember him—to remember the entire life he offered on behalf of the world. In sacrificing his Son, God gave his best for us. Jesus is God's best, not just because he is the Father's first and only begotten Son. He is God's best because he lived the best life that could possibly be lived. Israel's priests only accepted for sacrifice unblemished animals in their prime because the person making the offering was supposed to identify with the animal's exemplary life and reorient their life accordingly. Likewise, when we remember Christ at the Lord's table, we remember his exemplary life so we may order our lives accordingly.

Paul goes further in his reflection on the Lord's Supper. He reminds the Corinthians that, when we partake, we "proclaim the Lord's death until he comes" (1 Cor 11:26). This practice does not simply rehearse the passion events. Partaking in the Lord's Supper constitutes a faith statement about what the Lord's death accomplished—namely, reconciling all things to God. The Corinthians needed to be reminded of this because their shared meals proclaimed something altogether different. They partook of Christ's body and blood in a state of division with clear walls separating the haves and the have nots—to the point of humiliating the poor.[63] Since Christ broke down all such walls, any activity that rebuilds them contradicts the Lord's death. God judged the Corinthians for such hypocrisy, and some people even died as a result.[64]

Keeping the Lord's Table Central

As stewards of Christ's sacrifice, we must continue to keep the Lord's Supper at the center of our worship. It reminds us who gives us new life and the kind of new life he gives us. We break bread together because we live our new life in the context of kingdom community, as a part of the globally scattered body of Christ. To remove Christ's meal from the center of our worship creates a vacuum. That vacuum must be filled by something. If we are not intentional, some other center will usurp Christ's place, and our worship will be nullified. Many pseudo-centers vie for attention, including moral perfectionism, social activism, political agendas, personal experience, celebrity pastors, bibliolatry, and even the worship of worship. In their proper place, some of these are fairly harmless. When they occupy Christ's place, they all become idols.

Teaching and Accountability

Stewards of Christ's sacrifice remember his death in our teaching, preaching, and accountability. Christ gave his life for the whole world, and he asks us to give ours in kingdom service. But most of us don't really want to lay down our

---

63. 1 Cor 11:17–22.
64. 1 Cor 11:30–32.

lives. We don't want to place the needs of others before our own, but we will if we know that's what Christ requires. Preaching Christ's sacrifice with all of its personal, vertical, and horizontal dimensions helps keep our expectations properly calibrated. When we stop preaching and teaching Christ, we are tempted to preach and teach whatever sounds new or exciting. We tend to get sucked into the latest trends and prevailing philosophies.

If we want our formation in Christ to stick, we need to keep one another accountable. I may sound cynical, but most people, even good Christians, tend to follow the path of least resistance. We rise to the level of what others expect of us. If people don't check in with us about something, we tend to assume it's no longer necessary. For that reason, the author of Hebrews instructs us not to neglect meeting together but to encourage one another "all the more as you see the Day approaching" (Heb 10:25). Time is our friend insofar as it gives us opportunity to reach out to more people. Time is our foe insofar as we put off what is not pressing. The gospel implications of Christ's sacrifice are pressing for all who are lost. We need regular teaching, preaching, and accountability to keep that reality before us.

Forgiving

Finally, remembering Christ's sacrifice requires us to forgive one another. Jesus made quite clear, on multiple occasions, that accepting God's forgiveness requires extending forgiveness to others.

- For if you forgive others their trespasses, your heavenly Father will also forgive you; but if you do not forgive others, neither will your Father forgive your trespasses. (Matt 6:14–15)
- Then his lord summoned him and said to him, "You wicked slave! I forgave you all that debt because you pleaded with me. Should you not have had mercy on your fellow slave, as I had mercy on you?" And in anger his lord handed him over to be tortured until he would pay his entire debt. So my heavenly Father will also do to every one of you, if you do not forgive your brother or sister from your heart. (Matt 18:32–35)
- Whenever you stand praying, forgive, if you have anything against anyone; so that your Father in heaven may also forgive you your trespasses. (Mark 11:25)

Forgiveness comes as a group package. It includes membership in a fellowship of forgiven forgivers. When we stop forgiving others, we forfeit that membership. We've been given the ministry of reconciliation, which entails proclaiming the message of God's forgiveness. That act of proclamation makes us part of the forgiven and forgiving community. Withholding forgiveness means holding someone else hostage to sin. It erects a wall that Christ has torn down. It resurrects enmity that Christ has put to death on the cross. It crosses back over from the new age to the old age. Jesus did not mince words about forgiveness because failure to forgive is a deal breaker for him. We may not know exactly what Jesus meant by blasphemy of the Holy Spirit,[65] but holding people captive for whom Christ died when we hold the keys to their freedom is, clearly, an unforgiveable sin.

It doesn't matter how much we fight for the unborn, protest war, or seek pardon for those on death row. To withhold forgiveness negates all such efforts. We must continue to remember Christ's sacrifice in our preaching, teaching, accountability, and breaking bread, so we do not falter in this one crucial step—the step of forgiveness which could mean life or death for someone else. What the body of Christ binds on earth is truly bound in heaven.[66] When we grant forgiveness, God accepts it. That might sound more scandalous than necessary; God has already forgiven our offender. God has already reconciled all things to himself through Christ. Yet people must still accept his gift, repent from their sinful ways, and enter newness of life. If we stand between our enemies and the one who died for them, woe be unto us. As stewards of Christ's sacrifice, our most faithful act of service may be to free someone from their sin. It's what we were *re*born to do.[67]

---

65. Matt 12:31.

66. Matt 18:18.

67. For a clear and convicting account of forgiveness, see Johann Christoph Arnold, *Why Forgive?* (Maryknoll, NY: Orbis Books, 2013).

CHAPTER SEVEN

Bearing True Witness

PRIESTLY LEGACY

As Moses concludes his farewell address in Deuteronomy, he takes time to appoint his successors. Moses functioned as both leader and teacher for God's people. But he separates those roles for his successors. He appoints Joshua to lead the Israelites into the Promised Land and priests to instruct them in Torah and safeguard God's laws.[1] The Scriptures frequently refer to priests as teachers of the law. On numerous occasions, they were commissioned to teach it.[2] Ezra the priest was exemplary in this regard, "For Ezra had set his heart to study the law of the LORD, and to do it, and to teach the statutes and ordinances in Israel" (Ezra 7:10).[3] Israel's best kings reformed the Israelites according to Torah, and priests played a prominent role in those efforts.[4] King Hezekiah instructed the people to provide for the priests' economic needs precisely so they could devote themselves to Torah instruction.[5]

Should the priests fail to teach Torah, the results would be catastrophic for God's people. This is precisely what happened.[6] After detailing the Israelites'

---

1. Deut 17:18; 31:7–9; and 33:8–10.
2. They are called teachers in 2 Chron 15:3; Ezra 7:12, 21; Hag 2:11; and Mal 2:7. Various rulers commissioned them to teach that law in 2 Kgs 17:27; 2 Chron 19:8; Ezra 7:25; and Ezek 44:24.
3. Ezra was identified as both a priest and scribe in Ezra 7:11.
4. Jehoshaphat (2 Chron 19:8); Hezekiah (2 Chron 31:4); Josiah (2 Chron 34:14–33).
5. 2 Chron 31:4.
6. Mic 3:11; Jer 2:8; 18:18; and Ezek 7:26.

faithless, disloyal, ignorant ways, the prophet Hosea lays the blame squarely (though not exclusively) on the shoulders of their priests:

> Hear the word of the LORD, O people of Israel; for the LORD has an indictment against the inhabitants of the land. There is no faithfulness or loyalty, and no knowledge of God in the land. Swearing, lying, and murder, and stealing and adultery break out; bloodshed follows bloodshed. Therefore the land mourns, and all who live in it languish; together with the wild animals and the birds of the air, even the fish of the sea are perishing. Yet *let no one contend, and let none accuse, for with you is my contention, O priest.* You shall stumble by day; the prophet also shall stumble with you by night, and I will destroy your mother. My people are destroyed for lack of knowledge; because you have rejected knowledge, I reject you from being a priest to me. And *since you have forgotten the law* of your God, I also will forget your children. (Hos 4:1–6)

Priestly instruction is crucial because God intends to bless all nations through the life of a Torah-formed people. Should the Israelites order their lives according to God's designs for worship, fellowship, and stewardship, God would bless them generously and the nations would be drawn to God through them.

> See, just as the LORD my God has charged me, I now teach you statutes and ordinances for you to observe in the land that you are about to enter and occupy. You must observe them diligently, for this will show your wisdom and discernment to the peoples, who, when they hear all these statutes, will say, "Surely this great nation is a wise and discerning people!" For what other great nation has a god so near to it as the LORD our God is whenever we call to him? And what other great nation has statutes and ordinances as just as this entire law that I am setting before you today? (Deut 4:5–8)

Witness has always been central to salvation history. Since Abraham, God has been forming a people whose life together would show God's wisdom to all creation. God places that wisdom on display before the watching world in the life of his priestly people. After David established Jerusalem on Mount Zion as the nation's capital city and the place of God's dwelling, the notion of a "city on a hill" took on great meaning for God's people. The prophets envisioned the fulfillment of Israel's global mission in terms of nations streaming to Jerusalem for peace, justice, and Torah instruction.[7] Isaiah spells this out memorably,

> In days to come the mountain of the LORD'S house shall be established as the highest of the mountains, and shall be raised above the hills; all the nations shall stream to it. Many peoples shall come and say, "Come, let us go up to the mountain of the LORD, to the house of the God of Jacob; that he may teach us his ways and that we may walk in his paths." For out of Zion shall go forth instruction, and the word of the LORD from Jerusalem. He shall judge between the nations, and shall arbitrate for many peoples; they shall beat their swords into plowshares, and their spears into pruning hooks; nation shall not lift up sword against nation, neither shall they learn war any more. (Isa 2:1–4)

As in Deuteronomy 4, the nations express interest. What they see and hear impresses them, and they want to join God's people in embracing this abundant life. They come willingly and eagerly.

When the Babylonians ravaged Jerusalem, these prophecies appeared to have lost their significance. Jerusalem was no longer the capital of a thriving independent nation but a defeated territory managed by foreigners. Though God partially restored Jerusalem a few decades later, the dream of a hilltop city began to fade. When Babylon fell, the Persians ruled over the Promised Land and, after them, the Greeks and then Romans. Israel was no closer to becoming a glorious city that would spark the wider world's interest.

Jesus did not, however, forsake the hilltop city image. As he delivered his Sermon on the Mount, which extended Torah's relevance to the witness of his disciples, he recontextualized the city on a hill metaphor for its new messianic context:

> You are the salt of the earth; but if salt has lost its taste, how can its saltiness be restored? It is no longer good for anything, but is thrown out and trampled underfoot. You are the light of the world. A city built on a hill cannot be hid. No one after lighting a lamp puts it under the bushel basket, but on the lampstand, and it gives light to all in the house.

---

7. Isa 2:1–4; Jer 3:17; Micah 4:1–2; and Zech 8:22–23.

In the same way, let your light shine before others, so that they may see your good works and give glory to your Father in heaven. (Matt 5:13–16)

Rather than abandon the notion of a shining city, Jesus coupled it with the image of salt. His people would scatter like salt throughout the earth. And wherever they landed, they would shine like cities on a hill. The messianic mission would not revolve around one central city but numerous scattered cities. This scattering parallels the creation mandate to multiply and fill the earth. Paul takes this scattering in cosmic directions by comparing God's people to stars that shine throughout the universe.[8]

The point of these diverse metaphors remains the same: the core witness of all God's people, not just the Levites, consists of the peaceful way of life that God entrusted to us. Israel and the church's witness revolves around divinely ordained abundant life in harmony with the Creator and all creation. Though excessive entanglement and static residency could obstruct that mission, the absence of such things does not solely define their witness. If Israel's priests lived as exiles, harbored fugitives, and offered proper sacrifices, but failed to teach Torah, Israel's life and mission would fall apart—which is precisely what happened.[9] Likewise, should the church embrace our alien status, extend risky hospitality, and faithfully steward Christ's sacrifice without ordering our lives according to God's kingdom as revealed in Jesus, we too would fail at our central task. Displaying God's kingdom remains central to the church's mission, like keeping Torah defined Israelite witness.

RELATIONSHIP WITH GOD AND WORLD

To fully appreciate our relationship with God and world as pertains to our witnessing function, we must locate God's people within the story of creation, powers, and the people of God. God created this world and assumed responsibility for organizing everyday life. God refrains, however, from micromanaging his creation. He created humans in his image and commissioned them to fill the earth and exercise dominion over it. As humans multiplied and spread out, they needed organizational structures to coordinate their dominion efforts. So, God created a superstructure of

---

8. Phil 2:15.
9. Cf. 2 Chron 15:3–6 and Jer 2:8.

powers and principalities. They rule this world. As Colossians reminds us, God created these powers in and for Christ.[10] Their existence is not predicated solely upon human sinfulness; it is a necessary condition for human cooperation and thriving on a global scale. Some semblance of order would have been necessary even if there had been no fall. Hypothetically speaking, the powers could have developed in an entirely benevolent way to serve the good of humanity.

Of course, humanity did fall. And systems of order devolved into malevolent powers. Sin deeply impacted all creation, humans, and powers—resulting in violence, greed, discrimination, idolatry, pollution, exploitation, poverty, fornication, sickness, and death. This sorry *state* of affairs worsens as the powers regularly wield authority on loan from God to serve their own interests. Representative authorities include angels, kings, governors, public officials, utility providers, landlords, teachers, and parents. These powers function in erratic and unpredictable ways—sometimes serving and other times dominating, sometimes blessing and other times cursing. Though the world (including God's people) cannot function without these systems, they routinely perpetuate oppressive patterns of global domination.

Consequently, God uses these authorities for only limited purposes. Their self-interest ideally suits them for counteracting the self-interest of other powers. They thus keep one another in check and maintain a basic level of order throughout the world. But the powers cannot overcome the negative effects of sin and usher in a genuinely new and better order. As like begets like, orders rooted in self-interest only beget self-interested orders. Think of how the political left keeps the political right in check, and vice versa. Neither fully delivers on their own party's hopes and dreams, but they typically curb the worst excesses of the other.

God so loved the world that he wouldn't leave it in the hands of fallen powers. To usher in a new order of peaceful harmony, a different order of power is required. Through Christ, God formed his chosen people to represent that order. As sinners themselves, whose lives are deeply enmeshed in the old order, they cannot imagine, engineer, or otherwise inaugurate the new order. God himself must do that. God's people must serve as a sign to the world that the old order will not endure and that God's new order, his kingdom, will supplant it. To serve as a true sign of God's kingdom, his people must

---

10. Col 1:15–17.

learn that new order, arrange their lives by it, and extend God's invitation for all to enter it.

God revealed his perfect order through Christ. Since all creation came into being through him,[11] it follows that the way of Christ fulfills God's original intentions for creation. The way of Christ is how the world would have been had humans never sinned. It reveals the way things will someday be when Christ returns to complete the restoration of all things. God planned this from the beginning.[12] This explains why Christ deliberately fulfills Torah in his Sermon on the Mount.[13] God's instructions for Israel formed them in the way of Christ, in a contextually appropriate way, in preparation for his coming to complete their formation. God sent his Spirit to renew us in Christ's image and empower us for mission. Yet perfect adherence to God's kingdom is neither necessary nor possible—though some semblance is required for the sign to achieve its intended effect. As long as God's people continue initiating others into God's kingdom, which remains their purpose, these initiates will bring bits of the old order with them. God's people will thus never arrive at perfection without the kind of dramatic divine intervention anticipated in Daniel and Revelation.

In sum, God rules sovereignly over the everyday life of his creation. Sin has so distorted creation that the intended harmony was effectively fractured. Lest God's creatures devour one another in their sinfulness, God uses fallen world powers to maintain a tolerable degree of order throughout the earth. In God's hands, this old order provides enough stability for humanity's basic needs. But it cannot create the abundant life he intends for all creation. God has other plans for restoring his fallen creation and ushering in a genuinely new order of peace and well-being: the kingdom of God.

Since Abraham, God has been forming a people for himself who will inherit God's kingdom. Until the kingdom comes in full, they live to serve it. Their role does not involve maintaining the old fallen order but bearing witness to the new impending order. When God's people order their lives according to his reign, they serve as foretastes, first fruits, and demonstration plots of the coming kingdom. When the world looks at them, it catches a glimpse of the

---

11. John 1:1–4; Col 1:15–17; and Heb 1:1–2.
12. 1 Pet 1:19–21 and Eph 3:9–11.
13. Matt 5:17.

glorious future God has in store. Their embodied testimony serves as God's means of drawing all nations to himself.

Jesus didn't come to replace God's kingdom plan but to fulfill it. He brought the kingdom near and taught about it with authority. He lived it out perfectly and expanded its scope by incorporating Gentiles. Jesus broke the stranglehold sin and death had on creation. After gathering God's people, he instilled in them a vision of the kingdom that would propel them into mission. The church's role is to bear witness to the kingdom Christ revealed. That mission continues the vision that God began to instill in Israel through Torah. The intended effect remains one and the same: that the nations would come to God through the witness of his people.

IMPLICATIONS FOR THE CHURCH

Priestly witness encompasses every aspect of the church's life. For the world to see the church as a sign and foretaste of God's reign, our life together must point to God's ultimate intentions for all creation. Jesus authoritatively revealed God's kingdom, and the Holy Spirit guides and empowers the church to order its life accordingly. One way to discuss these implications involves compiling a list of the kingdom's attributes based on a careful study of the full New Testament witness to Christ.[14] For the sake of brevity, however, I take an approach that highlights the Levites' most concrete contribution to Israel's witness: their teaching of Torah. A fivefold schema derived from Torah sufficiently illuminates the formation of God's people in all ages.

God revealed the Torah to Israel to form them into a people whose life points to the way of Christ that was lost when Adam and Eve sinned. By analyzing the effects of the fall, we see five helpful categories that identify the kinds of problems Torah was designed to counteract. With respect to essence, we observe that (1) humans and (2) nonhuman creation suffer fragmentation in the form of death, degeneration, and decay. God answers such fragmentation with restoration. From a relational perspective, we observe friction in the form of distance, discord, and division between (3) humans and God, (4) humans and humans, and (5) humans and creation. God answers such friction with reconciliation, which results in properly ordered worship, fellowship, and stewardship.

---

14. Appendix 2 furnishes a list of kingdom characteristics based on this approach.

These five categories provide a helpful framework for unpacking Israel and the church's priestly witness to the world. I explore each one in turn.

Human Restoration

To the woman he said, "I will greatly increase your pangs in child-bearing; in pain you shall bring forth children." (Gen 3:16)

And to the man he said . . . "you are dust, and to dust you shall return." (Gen 3:17, 19)

The fall deeply impacted humanity in multiple ways. The consequences of sin in Genesis 3 are representative and not comprehensive.[15] Painful childbearing and death stand out among the worst. But they represent all manner of pain that humans experience on their journey toward death, including sickness, disease, physical deformity, and mental illness. Through Torah, God helped his people manage some of these negative consequences. The law gave women space and rest during their menstrual cycles. It contained skin diseases through isolation. Sabbath gave all humans the rest their bodies needed to rejuvenate and heal.[16] The prophets anticipated a day when the blind see, deaf hear, dumb speak, and lame walk.[17] When John the Baptist seeks confirmation that Jesus is the long-awaited Messiah, Jesus points to his healing ministry and highlights that the dead are raised.[18]

The theme of wholeness or well-being spans Scripture and serves as a sign of God's kingdom. Here I discuss five ways the church can point to and participate in God's healing work.

Praying for the Sick

Modern advances have made healthcare a staple of human society. People long to be whole, and the medical industry has done much to promote wellness. Christians certainly do not corner the market on healing and medicine,

---

15. For detailed analysis of all the fall's effects, see Nugent, *Genesis 1–11*, 59–63.
16. E.g., Lev 13–14; 18:19; and Deut 5:14–15.
17. Isa 35:5–6.
18. Matt 11:2–6.

but we have much to contribute. God's Spirit acts in our midst to promote supernatural healing and invites us to participate. The Spirit has gifted specific members of the body for this purpose.[19] God also desires to reveal his kingdom by answering our prayer for healing. James invites elders to lay hands on the sick and anoint them with oil that they may be healed.[20] Because God is powerful, there is power in prayer.

God does not always grant the healing for which we pray.[21] But praying persistently and thanking God abundantly for answered prayers serve as a powerful witness that God's kingdom brings wholeness where sin has brought sickness and death. Each healing God grants serves as a foretaste of resurrection life when the dead are raised. Only then does God promise to make us completely and irrevocably whole.

Meeting Physical Needs

God elects not to heal all people who pray for it. I suspect God has good reasons for this. For instance, the ubiquity of healing would probably undercut faith. All would recognize God's existence as a matter of regular experience. Faith would become sight and thus not faith at all. God also uses physical infirmities to display his power at work in weakness. God does not despise our injured humanity. He seeks to reveal his power through our weakness to overcome worldly human strength. God answered the apostle Paul's prayer for healing in this way, "My grace is sufficient for you, for power is made perfect in weakness." But, God didn't mean just any power. Paul embraced his own weakness so that "the power of Christ" would dwell in him (2 Cor 12:9).

Likewise, the church must not utterly despise weakness. Nor should we make light of people's pain and frustration. Rather, we come alongside one another to offer encouragement and help in times of need. God sometimes does powerful things directly through our weakness. My first back surgery, for example, opened the door for sharing the gospel with a dying man and his soon-to-be widow. God also does powerful things through the love of the Spirit-filled body of Christ. When people hunger, we feed them. When they cannot afford medicine or surgery, we give generously to supply their need.

---

19. 1 Cor 12:28.
20. Jas 5:14.
21. 2 Cor 12:7.

As far as it depends on us, we work toward the healing of our brothers and sisters, whatever it takes. This includes both calling upon God for supernatural deliverance and offering to be God's agent of natural forms of deliverance. Such love displays God's kingdom to a world with few resources beyond what their health insurance can cover and little hope that any good could come of their infirmity.

Visiting the Lonely

God observed early on in creation that "it is not good that the man should be alone" (Gen 2:18). We are social creatures, made for joy in fellowship and built for serving and loving others. It's unfortunate when a broken relationship results in loneliness and isolation. But isolation without conflict still violates God's design for human flourishing. Extended isolation begets and perpetuates various forms of mental illness and depression. Even those who appear to thrive in solitude do so at the expense of the rich communal life God intends for them.

The nuclear family helps safeguard people from complete loneliness, but it often falls short. God created us for fellowship with wider society—a fellowship that exposes us to the life-giving diversity of God's kingdom. Families can become insular and unhealthy, like a stagnant pond. And they will fail us. Family members die, move away, abuse us, and neglect even members who live close. So God enfolds us into his wider family. The body of Christ commits to visiting those who feel lonely, engaging them in meaningful fellowship, and activating their gifts for the good of others. The family of God offers companionship to those who are bedridden, imprisoned, or hospitalized and restores our sense of hope and belonging to the new humanity made possible in Christ. Such witness shines brightly in a world that increasingly turns people in on themselves and their electronic devices. The world flounders in its ignorance of what makes for true human flourishing.

Accommodating Infirmities

You have heard it said, "You shall not revile the deaf or put a stumbling block before the blind,"[22] but I say to you, learn sign language and envision a new

---

22. Lev 19:14.

world together with those who cannot see. Jesus did not actually say that last part, but it captures the spirit that should animate the body of Christ. The powers of this world can write legislation that obligates institutions and businesses to accommodate those who are differently abled. But such laws fail to integrate them into robust communal life where their unique abilities enrich the lives of others and, in so doing, become a source of joy and fulfillment for all.

The church goes further than the powers can. We come alongside brothers and sisters and combine our strengths and weaknesses so that all may participate fully in abundant kingdom life. Friendship Ministries provides one example of this.[23] Many churches gather regularly for an evening of songs, lessons, crafts, and games tailored specifically to those who are cognitively impaired. The program is not designed for them alone. The various activities provide a time of worship for all in an environment where the cognitively impaired excel and everyone grows. Our radical interdependence and inclusion challenges the world to reframe the notion of disability. It alerts them to the present reality of new creation where all people belong and contribute to a common good that encourages all.

Repenting from Self-Harm

God sent Christ that we might have abundant life.[24] We must come alongside others who suffer bodily in different ways. But we must also show regard for our own bodies. God did not make us whole so we could tear ourselves apart. Holistic witness to God's intentions means embracing healthy life rhythms that promote human flourishing.

Scripture warns against the sins of gluttony and drunkenness.[25] Such excesses both inflict damage upon our bodies and deprive others of the fellowship of which we should be capable. The community should strive to address the root causes that lead people to overeat and drink. But, as individuals, we should all strive to live exemplary lives in our bodies that reflect the high regard God has for our bodies. In Israel, a person could not serve as priest if they were physically deformed in some way, whether from birth

---

23. https://friendship.org
24. John 10:10.
25. Deut 21:20; Prov 23:20–21; 28:7; Luke 21:34; Rom 13:13; 1 Cor 5:11; 6:10; Gal 5:21; Eph 5:18; and 1 Pet 4:3.

or by accident. This law was not meant to demean those who suffered loss. Wholeness of body served as a visible image of the wholeness to which God calls his people and the wholeness he strives to foster among them. As God's priestly people, we should hold one another accountable for being good stewards of our bodies. We should also show wisdom and extend grace in cases of physical and mental illnesses beyond a person's control. Scripture and experience teach us that the body and spirit belong together. It is foolish, then, to focus on one to the neglect of the other.

Nonhuman Restoration

The LORD God said to the serpent, "Because you have done this, cursed are you among all animals and among all wild creatures; upon your belly you shall go, and dust you shall eat all the days of your life." (Gen 3:14)

And to the man he said . . . "cursed is the ground because of you . . . thorns and thistles it shall bring forth for you." (Gen 3:17–18)

The cursed serpent represents, among other things, the demotion of animals further below humans.[26] Combined, these two passages depict a cursed state for both animals and the soil. The deadly toll sin has taken upon them clearly emerges as the story continues. Immediately after the fall, God takes the life of an animal to provide clothing for the naked humans.[27] Cain then defiles the soil with Abel's blood.[28] After the flood, God places the fear of humans upon the animals, presumably because humans had excessively preyed upon them for sport and food.[29]

In Torah, God instructs his people to safeguard the well-being of nonhuman creation. Their farming and culinary practices honor the dignity of animals. Their war-making avoids running roughshod over forests. Their animals rest every seven days, and their land enjoys extended rest every seven years.[30] The prophets anticipate a day when animals live in peace and the curse is lifted from the soil.[31] In the New Testament, Paul links the redemption of humans

---

26. See Nugent, *Genesis*, 48–51.
27. Gen 3:21.
28. Gen 4:10–11.
29. Gen 9:2.
30. E.g., Deut 25:4; Gen 9:3–5; Exod 23:19; Deut 20:19; Exod 20:10; and Lev 25:4.
31. E.g., Isa 11:6; 65:25; Joel 2:21–22; 3:18; and Ezek 47:12.

to God's future restoration of all creation.[32] Scripture thus provides ample reasons why Christians should bear witness to God's ultimate intentions for nonhuman creation. Here I provide three practical suggestions.

Personal Stewardship

Torah gave abundant instructions as to how individuals should care for their animals, fields, and food. The New Testament nowhere suggests that Christians should do otherwise. To the extent that we farm land, we should treat our animals with utmost dignity and interact with our soil in ways that promote its well-being. We must not deplete the soil beyond repair for the sake of money, nor neglect our livestock for the sake of convenience. Rather, we practice humane animal husbandry in keeping with what best serves the animals themselves. We care for and do not neglect our pets. When we hunt, we respect our prey. We reject thinking, speaking, or treating them like clay pigeons. We do not consume animal blood, and we give thanks for the life of any creature we consume.

As far as it depends on us, we practice environmental care. We pay attention to the waste we generate, and we dispose of it carefully. We recycle joyfully even when we cannot be sure that our extra efforts will be game changers in the wider world's ecosystem. Our primary motive lies not in halting climate change or saving the environment, though we gladly do our part to help. We strive to bear witness to God's peaceable kingdom by affirming the goodness and inherent value of all creation. We set an example that others might follow even when it proves inconvenient and costly. We lay down our lives by putting the good of others before our own.

Corporate Stewardship

The church should not presume to hold its members accountable for creation care if the church itself does not set a positive example. Quite the opposite, the church collectively should exemplify creation stewardship for its members and spark their imaginations as to how they can participate. Our gathered lives should instruct and inspire our scattered lives in all things, including environmental concern.

---

32. Rom 8:18–24.

Churches with shared facilities and property possess many opportunities to showcase godly stewardship of land and natural resources to their members and neighbors. A church near me provides numerous receptacles for recycling paper, plastics, and glass throughout their building. Their parking lot hosts charging ports for eco-friendly vehicles—and not just for members. With such efforts, they don't quite reclaim the environment for Jesus, but they demonstrate their care for creation in ways that all can see. The church I am part of hosts multiple small groups that meet in homes each week to break bread. Though paper plates and plastic utensils allow for easier cleanup, we buy reusable dishes, silverware, and even communion glasses. Washing the dishes takes a bit more time, but we regard such time as worship. God is glorified by our efforts to care for his good creation.

The church should guard against allowing biblical practices like creation care to become politicized among God's people. Creation mattered to God and his people long before any political party appropriated it as a strategic platform. To prevent this, churches must be clear in their language and instruction. Practicing good stewardship is not enough, we must proclaim the glorified new creation to which we point with these practices. We must also be careful not to become disheartened when we cannot live this commitment out with absolute consistency. Creation care often costs more money and not all communities can equally afford it. In such cases, finding feasible ways to make our commitment visible is all the more important.

Pioneering Initiatives

No two churches are alike. They have different resources and opportunities. As churches explore how to creatively engage their community and bear witness to God's kingdom, they might choose to pioneer specific initiatives that show concern for nonhuman creation in their city. My church family adopted a community park in a rundown neighborhood where we had a strong presence. We did our best to keep it free of debris on behalf of the wider community, and we planted flowers to emphasize creation's beauty. Numerous opportunities exist to do that sort of thing. Other cities may provide unique opportunities to empower businesses or neighborhoods to recycle or increase energy efficiency. Christian volunteers can put in the extra time that others think they lack to care for their environment in practical ways.

Churches might also collaborate with neighborhood initiatives that already work in these ways. As Christians, we don't necessarily possess additional knowledge about which eco-friendly practices might yield the most fruit. But our care for God's good creation gives us an opportunity to be present among our neighbors. Our humility about what these endeavors might accomplish may be refreshing. Though we hope to make a difference, we recognize that regardless of our long-term ecological impact, our efforts point others to God's future restoration of all things. Our neighbors may be inspired that our commitment does not wane when we encounter obstacles, our efforts go unrecognized, and we cannot guarantee results. They may be drawn to our godly commitment to creation as a good in and of itself.

Reconciliation between Humans and Creation

The LORD God said to the serpent . . . "I will put enmity between you and the woman, and between your offspring and hers; he will strike your head, and you will strike his heel." (Gen 3:14–15)

And to the man he said . . . "cursed is the ground because of you; in toil you shall eat of it all the days of your life; thorns and thistles it shall bring forth for you; and you shall eat the plants of the field. By the sweat of your face you shall eat bread until you return to the ground, for out of it you were taken; you are dust, and to dust you shall return." (Gen 3:17–19)

Sin brought curses upon both the animals and the soil. These curses not only compromised creation's essence but disrupted the harmonious relationship humans originally shared with animals and the soil. We already discussed how Torah, the prophets, and the New Testament worked toward and anticipated the righting of these relationships. Here I briefly survey five common ways humans relate to the fallen world before suggesting a new approach that uniquely fits God's kingdom people.

Humans relate to nonhuman creation in a variety of ways, and they are not equal. The escapist believes that God plans to destroy this world and take his people to heaven. So how we relate to creation is ultimately insignificant. The survivalist believes this world is all we will ever have. So we must care for creation so as not to undercut the future existence of our own species. The animist believes this earth is quasi-divine, or at least equal to humans on the scale of being. So creation should be revered and cared for religiously. The creationist believes God created the earth as a good creation and placed humans above it to care for it on his behalf. The restorationist believes God began to restore this world through Jesus and invites us to join that work in anticipation of its ultimate completion.

I advocate a "new creationist" position, which requires more explanation.[33] It agrees with the restorationist that God will someday restore nonhuman creation fully. But the new creationist remains uncertain that this restoration has already begun. Rather, in Christ, God has begun a new creation in the midst of the old. God's kingdom people comprise that new creation. Yet the restoration of God's new humanity remains incomplete. We will realize our completion when nonhuman creation experiences restoration for the first time—when Jesus returns. In the meantime, we live in harmony with all creation in ways that anticipate the future harmony of God's full kingdom. When possible, we include nonhuman creation in the new creation life that we have already begun to experience. We eagerly include nonhuman creation in our new creation life that they might experience it secondhand through us. I base this new creationist position on a careful reading of Romans 8.

> For the creation waits with eager longing for the revealing of the children of God; for the creation was subjected to futility, not of its own will but by the will of the one who subjected it, in hope that the creation itself will be set free from its bondage to decay and will obtain the freedom of the glory of the children of God. We know that the whole creation has been groaning in labor pains until now; and not only the creation, but we ourselves, who have the first fruits of the Spirit, groan inwardly while we wait for adoption, the redemption of our bodies. (Rom 8:19–23)

Paul here depicts creation as longing not for its restoration but for the revelation of God's children. Creation knows that its freedom from decay depends upon the church's full freedom, which has already begun in part. God has already incorporated people into his new humanity, the first fruits of his Spirit, which serves as a down payment on God's fully restored new creation.[34] So, while God promises to restore all things, including nonhuman creation, this process has already begun for God's people in a way that it has not yet begun

---

33. See Nugent, *Endangered Gospel*, 16–18.
34. Eph 1:13–14.

for wider creation.[35] That being the case, God's people care for creation both by being exemplary stewards of it and by including it in the freedom, glory, and first fruits that have already begun with us. We thus care for creation like the creationist and work toward its improvement like the restorationist. Any responsible human should do that. But, as believers, we also do what only we can do: we include nonhuman creation in the new life that God has already begun among us through Christ.

Maintaining Community Gardens

Gardening has a way of schooling people in the ways of creation. As a naïve new homeowner, I knew what I wanted to plant around my house and how I wanted it to look. It certainly wasn't what the previous owner had left me. So, I yanked out all the old plants and attempted to build back better. Those with gardening experience know what's coming next. Most of what I planted didn't take. It turns out the soil is quite particular about what it wants to grow. Only certain plants thrive on certain plots of land. Soil composition, sunlight, temperature, winds, water level, insects, and wild critters all determine the possibilities. The gardener's desire proves to be least relevant in the long term. Good gardeners cooperate with the soil and plant accordingly. Gardening works as a two-way relationship in which neither party may simply impose its will on the other. What we learn from the soil teaches us about God's kingdom and even relationships between people.

Community gardens can take this relationship to another level. When believers fellowship together and open space in our lives and property for neighbors, we draw the soil into our fellowship. The garden becomes a site of kingdom living. Building friendships, teaching children, and sharing tools and produce become a cooperative endeavor in which the soil shares full partnership. How the co-op deals with critters and manages conflict is part of this shared experience. Those who spend a good deal of time working the soil also testify that they meet God there. He works in the creative forces governing all things. Those forces were at work before we got here, and they'll

---

35. Peter conveys this same idea, saying that Jesus remains in heaven until the universal restoration announced by the prophets begins (Acts 3:19–21). Nowhere in the New Testament do we have some sort of evidence that the curse has been lifted from the soil, the animals, or any facet of nonhuman creation. All language of already-but-not-yet salvation pertains to redeemed humans.

be working long after we're gone. Cooperating with them teaches us a lot about our own limited place in this world.

Worshipping Amid Creation

In numerous places, the Old Testament depicts the land mourning and suffering as humans reject God's ways and shed blood upon it.[36] How much more will the land rejoice when God's people love one another, give thanks to God, and exalt his name in its midst? Isaiah prophesied about this sort of thing:

> For you shall go out in joy,
>   and be led back in peace;
> the mountains and the hills before you
>   shall burst into song,
> and all the trees of the field shall clap their hands.
>   Instead of the thorn shall come up the cypress;
> instead of the brier shall come up the myrtle;
>   and it shall be to the LORD for a memorial,
>   for an everlasting sign that shall not be cut off. (Isa 55:12–13)

The well-being of God's chosen people serves the well-being of all creation. Our deliverance means renewed commitment to good stewardship of God's gifts and faithful witness to unbelieving neighbors. We do well to sing God's praises in our homes and in our sanctuaries, but we envelope nonhuman creation in that song when do so outdoors. As we join our voices with the sights and sounds of creation, we awaken our senses to God's good and beautiful creation. This, in turn, renews our commitment to godly stewardship. To praise God outdoors potentially garners the attention of our unbelieving neighbors and increases the surface area of our witness to God's intention for all creation.

Fellowshipping with Our Pets

Prophecies like Isaiah 55 employ poetic imagery that personifies the soil with human-like feelings. Scientifically speaking, the soil has no such feelings.

---

36. E.g., Num 35:33; Isa 33:9; Jer 12:4, 11; 23:10; Hos 4:3; and Joel 1:5–7.

But animals differ from the soil—especially higher functioning ones. While most of us don't interact with apes and dolphins on a regular basis, cats and dogs occupy prominent places in their owners' lives. Dogs especially tune in and even mirror the feelings of their owners. They can even be trained to offer sophisticated assistance in times of distress. They are thus quite capable of experiencing joy in fellowship. Dogs can be conditioned to protect their owners and threaten or maim any intruder. They can discriminate based on appearance, sound, and smell. In so doing, dogs learn the old order language of the powers and principalities, keeping hostile forces at bay so their own pack can flourish.

How much more can dogs learn the new order language of God's kingdom! They can be trained to welcome strangers, roughhouse with their owners, act gently around children, and help those who are frail. They can even get excited and celebrate with us during parties. Most dogs will do so primarily with members of their household, but they can also celebrate enthusiastically with the wider kingdom community. They can learn to love people from a wide variety of ethnicities, walks of life, political leanings, abilities, and preferences. They thus learn at least some of the language of God's kingdom.

I experienced this a while back with my golden retriever, Reese. We hosted several yard and pool parties with dozens of families from church and a good number of students from the college where I teach. Reese fed off the energy as he bounced from person to person being petted, fed, and spoken to as if he were one of us. He would patrol the pool's edge looking for people in distress and soaking in random splashes of water and deliberate attention from people playing and laughing. Reese experienced kingdom life as few dedicated watchdogs ever do. The energy he drew and then radiated to others bore witness to God's work in our lives and thus to a kingdom he could never fully understand but certainly grew to appreciate.

Reconciliation between Humans and Humans

> To the woman he said . . . "your desire shall be for your husband, and he shall rule over you." (Gen 3:16)

At the time of the fall, Genesis depicts Adam and Eve as the only two people on earth. The account therefore depicts the friction that sin generates between humans in terms of husband-and-wife relations, and it's not good. We cannot be certain what the text means by the woman's "desire." Perhaps she reaches

131

out to her husband in her pain, and he takes advantage of her vulnerability by asserting his dominance. Regardless, the second half of verse 16 conveys a power struggle. Like other aspects of the fall, this struggle represents a broader struggle between humans. We see this struggle between strong men and weak men, free women and slave women, majority and minority, kings and commoners, old and young, citizens and aliens, and so forth. Whenever people sense they have an advantage, they use it to assert their dominance. This results in widespread social disharmony, violence, exploitation, and servitude.

Torah counteracts social upheaval by dispersing power among a plurality of leaders, condemning all exploitation of the poor, protecting vulnerable women and children, upholding the dignity of servants and aliens, and honoring parents in their old age.[37] The prophets criticize God's people for rejecting this benevolent social ethic and anticipate a day when the high and mighty are brought low while the low are raised up.[38] Jesus proclaimed his kingdom as the fulfillment of this hope.[39] On the cross, he broke down the wall of separation that divides people and created a new humanity that makes no distinctions based on accidents of birth.[40] When the kingdom comes in full, this will be the way of all creation.

Though Christ has broken down the wall of division, once and for all, we live in a day when division prevails in nearly every aspect of life. Race remains a perennial problem. Men and women continually struggle over power. Civil dialogue between people of diverse political persuasions seems impossible. The church is thus ideally suited to bear witness to an alternative kingdom of true equality and unity amid diversity. In chapters 5 and 6, I discussed practices of hospitality and reconciliation that go a long way to unite believers in conflict. Here I focus on four areas where the church's witness shines brightly by embodying the social vision of God's kingdom, which remains as radical now as it was in the first century.

Diverse Membership

Believers must affirm that all people are equal in God's eyes and that Christ has broken down the wall of separation that divides us. But if our life together

---

37. E.g., Deut 16–18; Exod 22:25; 23:6, 11; Deut 15:11; 24:17; 26:12–13; and Exod 20:12.
38. E.g., Amos 2:6–8 and Isa 5:7–18.
39. E.g., Luke 4:16–21.
40. E.g., Eph 2:11–21; Gal 3:28 and Col 3:11.

as a church family does not display unity across diversity, then we are merely paying lip service. Such diversity is easier said than done. The choices we make about location, building type, preacher, worship style, and music all tend to predetermine what types of people gravitate toward us and stick around long term. Since like begets like, we continue to attract the same sort of people.

This challenge is difficult to overcome. Nonetheless, we should be deliberate about the choices we make. We must avoid the temptation to maximize our growth potential by harnessing the like-begets-like principle to target and become a church for a narrow demographic niche. A church may strive for kingdom diversity and fall short. But failing in that effort is better than striving for worldly growth through deliberate homogeneity and succeeding. Keeping the struggle alive and trying every idea we can imagine at least communicates our kingdom values and ambition.

We should also avoid judging our commitment to diversity by the social issue that is most pressing in the media at the current moment. Diversity involves more than skin color. And different regions are diverse in different ways. A more important question might be, who are the diverse people of our community who should be attracted to the kingdom Jesus brought? Do the poor, those of low account, sinners, outcasts, and social misfits find a home among us? If rich people from a variety of ethnic backgrounds are entirely comfortable, but poor people are not, then our diversity may differ from that for which Jesus died.

Economic Sharing

Diversity of economic standing bears great weight since financial well-being presents one of the most significant forms of witness. Torah, the prophets, Jesus, Acts, and New Testament letters all highlight the radical economic vision God casts for his people. The powers have always failed to uphold an order of economic justice in which poor people do not fall through the cracks, or they succeed at meeting needs only at the expense of people's dignity. God called both Israel and the church to radical generosity and economic sharing. While the powers rule erratically, the good news of a kingdom people who meet needs respectfully and raise people from their lowly status should appeal to those who are struggling financially.

Those with greater financial means also share a role in the kingdom community. They lower themselves economically and socially in order to elevate the status of those who are usually stuck at the bottom. Such voluntary inversion liberates the wealthy from bondage to stuff and status. Their relative economic stability need not be an anchor that drags them down. It should become a point of stability for the wider community. When others experience tough times, wealthier members are perfectly positioned to help. When someone needs transportation, more prosperous members may have a vehicle to share. They enable borrowers to live on a comparatively lower income while still getting around as needed. Generous sharing generates goodwill between believers from diverse walks of life. It also bears witness to a kingdom in which God not only meets all needs but supplants an economics of scarcity with an economics of abundance.

Power Inversion

Achieving diverse membership and fostering an economics of abundance through generous giving and sharing go a long way to cultivating the social vision of Jesus. But if those with wealth continue wielding power over members of lower economic standing in the kingdom community, then the church still mirrors the diversity and economics of fallen society. That may be progress, but it's not quite God's kingdom. Wider society typically balances power by replacing a homogeneous group of powerful people who control the community conservatively with a mixed group of powerful people who do the same thing more progressively. In both cases the fallen order of domination endures.

Jesus transcended this power struggle by envisioning a kingdom in which the first are last, the great are least, the low are raised and the rich lowered, the less honorable receive more honor, and leaders serve rather than rule over the body.[41] Jesus makes this power inversion possible by pouring his Spirit upon all members. Joel foresaw that God's Spirit would be the great equalizer: "Then afterward I will pour out my spirit on all flesh; your sons and your daughters shall prophesy, your old men shall dream dreams, and your young men shall see visions. Even on the male and female slaves, in those days, I will pour out my spirit" (Joel 2:28–29). Peter recognized on the day of Pentecost that God had begun this very thing.[42] Since the church is

---

41. Matt 19:30; 20:1–16; Mark 9:35; 10:31; Luke 13:30; Jas 1:9–10; 1 Cor 12:22–26; and Mark 10:42–45.

42. Acts 2:14–21.

animated by God's Spirit and since Christ pours his Spirit on all members, the voice of every member matters greatly. God may speak through any member he wishes. It seems more expedient to bypass a congregation-wide listening process and relinquish all important decisions to an elected board of powerful people. But the resulting structure hardly bears witness to the kingdom Jesus brought and the power inversion that made his kingdom so revolutionary and life-giving.

Universality of Gifts

Should the Church embrace its diversity, level the playing field economically, and heed the unique voice of each member, it would be well on its way to a robust kingdom vision. But one more shift remains. In a community where every need is met and every voice is heard, people can still wield excessive power by performing most of the ministry that takes place within the body. Churches often grant great power to those who out-serve everyone else. This, too, results in a subtle form of domination. Monopolizing opportunities to serve keeps certain people in the perpetual position of dependents who only take and never give. This robs them of their dignity and agency.

God addresses this problem, again, by sending his Spirit. God's Spirit endows each member with a gift or means of service.[43] Paul describes a healthy church body in terms of leaders who equip all members for service to build up the body. Leaders must continue to do so until the whole body comes to

> "the unity of the faith and the knowledge of the Son of God, to maturity, to the measure of the full stature of Christ. We must no longer be children, tossed to and fro and blown about by every wind of doctrine, by people's trickery, by their craftiness in deceitful scheming. But speaking the truth in love, we must grow up in every way into him who is the head, into Christ, from whom the whole body, joined and knit together by every ligament with which it is equipped, as each part is working properly, promotes the body's growth in building itself up in love." (Eph. 4:13–16)

---

43. Cf. Rom 12:4–8; 1 Cor 12:7–13; 14:26; Eph 4:11–13; and 1 Pet 2:4–9. Paul prefers the word "grace" or "charism" from which we get the term charismatic.

In God's kingdom all people lay down their lives for others. All people place the needs of others before their own. Such generosity is key to abundant living. Such love participates in Christ's own condescension to serve humanity.[44]

Where the gifts of the many remain inactive, power and influence are hoarded by few. God broke down the wall of division and domination, and the church responds by providing for each member's needs, heeding each member's voice, and activating each member for kingdom service. Participation in Spirit-empowered service positions believers to experience life transformation that only those yielded to the way of Christ and committed to the good of others can experience. This kind of robust social witness is entirely absent from the bland utopias of the powers and principalities. It should, therefore, stand out among our unbelieving neighbors for its new creation pioneering power.

Reconciliation between Humans and God

> They heard the sound of the LORD God walking in the garden at the time of the evening breeze, and the man and his wife hid themselves from the presence of the LORD God among the trees of the garden. But the LORD God called to the man, and said to him, "Where are you?" He said, "I heard the sound of you in the garden, and I was afraid, because I was naked; and I hid myself." (Gen 3:8–10)

When God confronts Adam and Eve for sinning, the consequences he lists pertain to the sinners, the serpent, and the soil. The three-part judgment poem of Genesis 3 says nothing about God's relationship with the first two humans, but something has clearly changed. When Adam and Eve hear God coming, they hide in fear. Disobedience begets insecurity and a host of negative consequences.

Almost immediately afterward, God showers them with grace. He makes garments of skin and clothes them, and then he sends them out of the garden. This sending could be interpreted as a breach of fellowship, but it need not be. We often assume that God and humans routinely hung out together in the garden and that God no longer wants to play. But the text doesn't say that. It says that God drove them out because they knew good and evil, and access to

---

44. Phil 2.

the tree of life in such a state would be a bad idea. In sealing off the entrance, God makes clear that they no longer had access to the tree of life. It says nothing about access to God himself. In fact, the very next chapter depicts Eve giving birth to Cain "with the help of the Lord." We see God interacting with Cain and Abel, God advising Cain how to deal with his anger issues, and God intervening again after Cain kills Abel. God then appears to forgive Cain for his offense and protects him when the consequences of his actions seemed too much for him to bear.[45]

Though humans reject God's life-giving instructions for them, he consistently strives to make amends with them. In love, he disciplines them, but always for their well-being.[46] God originally conveys his will for right worship in Torah. The prophets clarify God's will over and against Israel's disobedience. Then Jesus most fully reveals God's will when he takes on flesh. Here I discuss three ways God's people bear witness to a right relationship with God. This list is incomplete insofar as a right relationship with God includes many more practices, and much more can be said about these three practices themselves. I thus submit what follows as a brief introduction to three representative practices that help foster a right relationship with God. Through them God's priestly people might show the world what right relationship with God looks like.

Reading Consistently

When God introduces himself to Moses, Moses asks to know God's name.[47] Exchanging names usually marks the first step in getting to know someone. What a critical moment in salvation history! God seized this opportunity and set the stage for all future generations who would come to know him. God identifies himself as "I am who I am" or "I will be who I will be." God is not a man with a name that gives us a handle on who he is. Rather, God is the one who is who he is. One gets to know God by witnessing his acts in history. It's as if God said, "Follow me and you'll learn who I am."

The same holds true for us today. To know God truly we must follow him. Unlike Moses, however, we come late to God's saving acts in world history. He's been revealing himself to his chosen people for over three thousand

---

45. Gen 4:1–15.
46. Deut 8:5; Prov 3:11–12; Heb 12:5–11; and Rev 3:19.
47. Exod 3:13–15.

years, and he has revealed himself most fully in Jesus. Right relationship with him requires familiarizing ourselves with that revelation, which is preserved for us in Scripture. Nothing can substitute for reading the Bible. Immersing ourselves in God's word on a regular basis schools our understanding and corrects our faulty beliefs. It directs us away from idolatry and places us on a path of faithfulness. Daily Bible reading is great, but studying Scripture in community with fellow believers is better. The assistance of gifted teachers enriches our daily reading and helps curtail poor interpretations.

Scripture furnishes the criteria by which we judge all other claims about God, his will for this world, and our lives within it. Reading Scripture does not itself create a right relationship with God. Absorbing his word without acting upon it proves futile, like looking in a mirror and forgetting what we look like.[48] Scripture reveals God to us and summons us to right relationship with him. That relationship grows as we enter the story of Scripture at our point in salvation history. Because God's word is living and active, it is more than words on a page. As we read those words, God speaks to us through his Spirit with an immediacy that transcends the letters and enters into the specificity of our minds and lives. Many people complain that God does not speak to them. Reading Scripture on a regular basis with eyes, ears, and hearts open positions oneself for faith-enriching, life-transforming conversation.

Praying Obediently

Prayer and Scripture reading go hand in hand. In prayer, we set our lives before God and in Scripture he reveals his life to us. We should not think of prayer as informing God about our lives, as if he doesn't already know what's going on.[49] Rather, in prayer, we offer our lives to God, to do with as he wills. It's why Jesus taught us to pray, "Your kingdom come your will be done, on earth as it is in heaven" (Matt 6:10). It's why Jesus himself prayed in the garden of Gethsemane that he'd endure even the cross if that's what God wants. When conversing with God, we calibrate our wills to his. Jesus instructs us to seek God's kingdom above all things.[50] So we pray kingdom prayers. We ask God to provide our needs as we seek his kingdom. We petition him to protect us from evil and to empower us for service as we do his will.

---

48. Cf. Jas 1:22–25.
49. Matt 6:8.
50. Matt 6:33.

Prayer remains crucial because doing God's will is central to a right relationship with him. God desires us to order our entire lives according to his will.[51] This sort of arrangement is unhealthy with other humans, but not with God, for he alone truly knows and wills what is best for us and the whole world. He wills our flourishing. He wills our inclusion in his kingdom work. Such work holds the key to abundant life and the future of world history. Those who do God's will live forever.[52] Recognizing this, our prayer often issues in thanksgiving and praise. God's people have thus long enjoyed singing their prayers together.

Like Scripture reading, prayer also opens the door for God to speak to us through his Holy Spirit. In prayer, we commune with God, setting aside all other productive activity. In that moment, we prioritize him above all things. As with Scripture, prayer itself does not constitute our relationship with God. A necessary connection does not exist between the amount of time and words spent praying and the strength of our faith. Rather, when we pray as those who strive to align our lives with God's will and when we act in accordance with God's word to us, we enter into abundant life in him. We heed the words of the priest Eli who instructed young Samuel to pray, "Speak, Lord, for your servant is listening" (1 Sam 3:9).

Loving Holistically

A person's bloodstream delivers all the oxygen, nutrients, and hormones that a healthy body needs to function. It also removes harmful waste, such as carbon dioxide. Like veins and arteries taking blood to and from our heart, praying and reading Scripture circulates the lifegiving divine word among those longing for a healthy relationship with God. But a person does not exist so their circulatory system might perform this service. Rather, it performs this service so all the body's parts might work together to accomplish the person's will. So it is with the body of Christ and all of its members. Prayer and Scripture enable us to do God's will, which is to love.

The teachers of the law were committed to prayer and Scripture, but they wanted to know what Jesus thought a good Jew should do above all.[53] They probably knew that Jesus willed God's kingdom, but what aspects

---

51. 1 Pet 4:2.
52. 1 John 2:17.
53. Matt 22:34–40.

of God's kingdom should his followers prioritize? As Torah-observant Jews, they asked this question in terms of Torah: What is the greatest commandment in the law? Jesus provided a two-pronged answer: love God and love your neighbor. This answer lies at the heart of a right relationship with God.

The connection between love of God and love of neighbor stands out in this answer. For Jesus, one does not love others only as a result of loving God; one loves God precisely in the process of loving others.[54] Jesus articulated this in his parable of the sheep and goats, saying, "just as you did it to one of the least of these who are members of my family, you did it to me" (Matt 25:40). He impressed this upon Peter three times, insisting that if Peter loved him, then Peter would feed his sheep.[55] Jesus also implied as much when he introduced himself to Saul, the Christian killer, as "Jesus, whom you are persecuting" (Acts 9:5). Saul never met Jesus; he had only persecuted his disciples. In attacking them, he attacked Jesus. John derives this same meaning from Jesus's twofold love commandment, saying, "Those who say, 'I love God,' and hate their brothers or sisters, are liars; for those who do not love a brother or sister whom they have seen, cannot love God whom they have not seen. The commandment we have from him is this: those who love God must love their brothers and sisters also" (1 John 4:20–21).

These passages clarify that right relationship with God may not be reduced to fervent acts of vertical piety. Those have their place, but not to the exclusion of love for fellow humans, particularly brothers and sisters in Christ. As faith without works is dead, so love of God without love of neighbors falls flat. Nor will it do to love only those who are easy to love. We must extend love to the least of God's family, to those who cannot repay us, and even to our enemies and persecutors. In this way, we are children of God.[56] In all of these ways we are priests of God Most High.

---

54. David Augsburger develops this theme at length in *Dissident Discipleship: A Spirituality of Self-Surrender, Love of God, and Love of Neighbor* (Grand Rapids: Baker, 2006).

55. John 21:15–17.

56. Matt 5:45.

CHAPTER EIGHT

The Politics of Praise

PRIESTLY LEGACY

God reveals his will for Israel's priests in Torah, the first five books of the Old Testament. Until now, the four priestly responsibilities we've discussed have been firmly rooted in the stories and legislation of Torah. When it comes to musical praise, however, Torah says surprisingly little. The most we can say is that certain priests were responsible for blowing trumpets to assemble the Israelites, whether for war, festivals, or general assemblies.[1] Though Israel likely sang songs of praise during various festivals, Torah nowhere specifies that priests led out in this capacity.

Israel's priests appear to have taken on musical responsibilities during the monarchy, and it appears to have been David's idea. From his early days in the court, we see that David made beautiful music. He played the lyre to comfort King Saul whenever an evil spirit came upon him.[2] But how did performing music evolve from the personal passion and skill of David to a priestly responsibility? To answer this question, we turn to events in the early years of David's reign, as narrated in 1 Chronicles.

After consolidating his reign over Israel, King David sought to bring the ark of the covenant to Jerusalem, his newly christened capital. The ark's caretakers, who were apparently not priests, placed it on a new cart and began transporting it. *All of Israel* celebrated "with song and lyres and harps and tambourines and cymbals and trumpets" (1 Chron 13:8). The festivities

---

1. Num 10:10.
2. 1 Sam 16:23.

ended abruptly, however, when the cart struck a rock, the ark toppled, and God struck its courier dead for reaching out to stabilize it.

David had neither inquired properly of the Lord before moving the ark nor followed Torah's instructions regarding its care. Only priests may care for and transport the ark. And they must do so by running long poles through the ark's rings and then carrying those poles upon their shoulders at a reverent distance.[3] In anger, and probably shame, David abandoned the ark project and left it in the house of a Philistine. Sometime later, he inquired properly of the Lord before engaging the Philistines in two important battles. God gave him permission and victory. Bolstered by the success of these campaigns, David resolved to give the ark another try. This time, he made sure the Levites alone carried the ark according to all the instructions of Moses.[4] Furthermore, going above and beyond Torah's requirements, he commissioned head Levites to appoint musicians and singers from among their kindred "to raise loud sounds of joy" (1 Chron 15:16). Apparently, David didn't want to take any more chances. This time, he commissioned Levites to lead out in all aspects, including song. And the procession was a great success.

Pleased with the outcome, David made Levitical singing a permanent institution: "on that day David first appointed the singing of praises to the LORD by Asaph [a Levite] and his kindred" (1 Chron 16:7). He also appointed specific Levites to tend to the ark on an ongoing basis and to give thanks to God in sacred song and instrumental accompaniment.[5] By the time David transferred his kingdom to his son, Solomon, over one-tenth of the Levites specialized in offering praise accompanied by musical instruments.[6] This function helped occupy the sons of Levi who could no longer look after the mobile tabernacle since Solomon replaced it with a stationary temple, at David's behest.[7]

All of these events seem relatively innocent. "See how much David loves God!" we might observe. However, his delegation of musical responsibilities to the Levites belies a profound domestication of the priesthood.

According to Moses, should the Israelites desire a king, that king must make his own copy of the law in the presence of priests. Presumably, this

---

3. Exod 25:14–15; 37:5; Deut 10:8; and 1 Chron 15:15.
4. 1 Chron 15:15.
5. 1 Chron 16:37–43.
6. 1 Chron 23:3–5.
7. 1 Chron 23:25–26.

meant the king should lead by administering the dictates of Torah rather than doing what seems right in his own eyes or embracing kingship like the nations. Like Saul before him, however, David abandoned the radical political and social vision of Torah and replaced it with worldly economics and politics. David's standing army obviated God's miraculous deliverance. David's capital city eradicated the equality of all Israelite tribes. David and Solomon's stationary temple supplanted God's intentionally mobile shrine. The tabernacle could no longer follow where God's presence led. The ark could no longer lead God's people in war. In fact, David initially consulted military commanders *and not priests* before deciding what to do with the ark.[8] Israel was becoming a worldly empire, a military state.

This meant the end of Israelite priesthood as set forth in Torah. Priests no longer monitored Israel's economics and politics; the king did. They no longer spoke the final word on potential wars; the king did. From then on, the king settled all matters that stumped local rulers, eclipsing the role of Israel's high priests via Urim and Thummim. Perhaps cities of refuge never caught on because swift royal justice replaced patient priestly hospitality. Though priests still occupied prominent positions in the temple and sacrificial system, Israel's kings added non-Levites to their ranks as well. The kings submitted some of their own offerings and commandeered the priestly ephod on occasion.[9] To make matters worse, some priests even prophesied "under the direction of the king."[10] Though we cannot be sure exactly what that meant, at a minimum the practice suggests that Israel's kings placed priests under their jurisdiction rather than beside them. God's divinely appointed priests were meant to serve alongside Israel's kings to discern and uphold God's will for Israel. It appears, then, Israel's kings had largely domesticated the Levites and then compensated for that by giving them high-profile posts as court musicians.[11]

---

8. 1 Chron 13:1.

9. E.g., 2 Sam 8:17–18 (David's sons serve as priests); 2 Sam 20:25–26 (Ira, from the tribe of Manasseh, served as David's private priest; cf. Num 32:41 and Deut 3:14); and Ezra 2:40–50 (a list of priests contains the servants of Solomon, which appears to be a non-Levitical group). Saul offers a sacrifice to consecrate a war (1 Sam 13:9) and Solomon offers incense to God at various high places (1 Kgs 3:3). David wears an ephod in 2 Sam 6:14 and 1 Chron 15:27 and uses an ephod to inquire of the Lord in 1 Sam 30:7–8.

10. 1 Chron 25:2.

11. Second Chronicles 29:25 notes that David appointed Levites to the house of the Lord with instruments as a divine command through the prophets. We have no record of this command, but that doesn't mean it didn't happen. Nor does it mean that the kings did not domesticate Israel's priests. It could simply be another concession that God made

We may be tempted to think that the priests just rolled over and accepted this sorry fate. However, Scripture contains much evidence to the contrary. It turns out, the pen is truly mightier than the sword. With their newly diminished role and considerably more time on their hands, several priests took to composing. They wrote a series of historical books known as the Chronicler's history (1 Chronicles—Nehemiah), which records the deeds of Israel's kings and prophets from a priestly perspective. We learn a good deal about the domestication of Israel's priests from this unique historical record. Other priests, like Jeremiah and Ezekiel, served as prophets and drafted (with help) some of the most scathing criticisms of both the wicked kings and the sellout priests who prostituted themselves before those kings.

Finally, they wrote songs. Though a good number of songs in the book of Psalms are associated with David and others remain anonymous, two collections are attributed specifically to priests—namely, Asaph and Korah.[12] Israel's priests likely played an important role in the composition and shaping of the Psalter, even psalms associated with David. The phrase "A Psalm of David," which is affixed to nearly half the psalms, could mean that David wrote the song, commissioned the song, included the song in his collection, or was the subject of the psalm. We shouldn't assume that David wrote all songs associated with him. Nor should we assume that the songs David actually wrote were written without the help of his professional court musicians, the Levites.

Whatever the precise relationship between David and various psalms, the Psalter represents the critical intersection of priests and world powers. As such, they provide a unique perspective on how God's people might speak and bear witness to world powers who still seek to domesticate God's priestly people. Read in this light, the psalms speak a bold yet respectful word to people in high places who have clearly drifted from God's intentions for them. From this perspective, it is remarkable that many of these subversive songs were written by or under the auspices of David. They confess the absolute sovereignty of the very God who threatens to undermine the entire royal enterprise. Of course, not all songs are subversive, and that too is relevant. When speaking

---

to Israel's misguided choice to crown a king like the nations and build a capital city with a stationary temple like the nations. If God is going to allow a stationary temple, then the priests should lead its musical worship as they do sacrificial worship. It may not be God's original design for Israel's sacred space, but it still remains sacred.

12. For Asaph, see Pss 50, 73–83. For the sons of Korah, see Pss 42, 44–49, 84–85, 87–88.

a liberating word in captivity, subtlety is paramount. Testimony that is always and only critical quickly falls on deaf ears.

I will not sift through each psalm and draw out all their subversive sentiments, but a representative sampling is instructive.[13] Among Asaph's songs, we read that Israel's God cuts off princes and inspires fear in kings.[14] We read that God alone holds power to deliver his people from the nations.[15] We learn that God stands in judgment of both earthly kings and heavenly rulers who wield authority and bear responsibility for the nations.[16] Various songs of the Korahites repeatedly affirm that God is king,[17] that he alone is our refuge,[18] and that sword and bow cannot be trusted.[19] They assert that wealth leads to folly[20] and that one day in God's courts is better than thousands anywhere else (i.e., the courts of human kings).[21]

Such lyrics are not unique to the songs associated with named priests. They permeate the entire psalter.[22] In fact, some scholars suspect that the book of Psalms was organized to highlight the failure of Israel's kingship and the ultimate triumph of God's unmediated reign over his people.[23] That these songs were written under the noses of Israel's kings and foreign emperors testifies to the power of their subtlety. In keeping with Torah, these poets upheld the unrivaled kingship of Israel's God amid Israel's monarchy, which had orchestrated the structural rejection of Torah. Such songs chastened any king's delusions of unquestioned sovereignty. Framed as praise to Israel's God, they managed to fly under the radar even while being sung in the royal

---

13. For an analysis of subversives singing in the New Testament, see R. Alan Streett, *Songs of Resistance: Challenging Caesar and Empire* (Eugene, OR: Cascade Books, 2022).

14. Ps 76:12.

15. Pss 48, 79–83.

16. Ps 82.

17. Ps 44:4; 47:2; and 84:3.

18. Pss 46–47.

19. Ps 44:5–7

20. Ps 49.

21. Ps 84:10.

22. Consider that Pss 2–10, most of which are associated with David, call all kings to fear God, express radical trust in God and not troops, identify God as king, confess God as the standard of righteousness, affirm shared dominion of humans over creation, place God above all nations, and announce that God will judge nations according to his standards of justice. Ps 9 is an excellent case study of a song that speaks truth about power.

23. Cf. Gerald Henry Wilson, *Editing of the Hebrew Psalter*, Society of Biblical Literature Dissertation Series (Chico, CA: Scholars, 1985) and "The Shape of the Book of Psalms," *Interpretation* 46 (1992): 129–142.

court during nationwide festivals. Many songs chafed against various kings' aspirations, but even the king couldn't question central tenets of Israelite faith. The people would revolt.

The Book of Psalms is hardly a civil religion songbook. It would be extremely difficult to argue they were merely applying a veneer of religiosity to the king's power and using God's name to bolster royal fame. Quite the contrary, many songs that uphold Israel's kings and the Davidic dynasty do so in ways that subsume them under the larger story of God's deliverance of Israel throughout salvation history.[24] In subordinating the royal to the divine in this way, these psalms anticipate Jesus's words to Pilate: "You would have no power over me unless it had been given you from above" (John 19:11).

RELATING TO GOD AND WORLD

You are a chosen race, a royal priesthood, a holy nation, God's own people, *in order that you may proclaim the mighty acts of him* who called you out of darkness into his marvelous light. (1 Pet 2:9)

When it comes to praise, Israel's priests confessed their God as Lord and King of all creation. He is Lord of life and death, Lord over nations and heavenly hosts. By his mighty acts, God delivered his people Israel. He is the only sure refuge in times of trouble. He alone is worthy of all praise. We relate to him from a posture of awe, appreciation, trust, and obedience. As believers, we confess that God has made himself known through Jesus Christ. In faith, we confess him as Lord and Savior, King of kings, the one through whom all creation came into being. He sits at God's right hand with all rulers and authorities in heaven and on earth being subjugated under his feet. Through Jesus, all God's purposes for creation find their fulfillment. By his mighty acts, God brings human history toward its appointed end.

The lordship of Jesus therefore impacts all we say and do among ourselves and in relation to the world. He is Lord in all circumstances, no matter what we are going through. He is Lord in all company, no matter who we are with; Lord of all life, supreme over every dimension of creaturely existence. He is Lord in all places, such that his reign relates to every corner of the globe—every

---

24. E.g., Ps 78.

village, city, and state capital. In all conceivable times, places, company, and spheres of life—both private and public—we have been called to represent his eternal unshakeable kingdom as priests and ambassadors.

This posture of praise must frame every aspect of our relationship to the world. And it may just help us break through the impasse of how we should speak to unbelievers who hold authority over us. It gives us insight as to what we might say and how we might say it. For these authorities often strive to domesticate us, as Israel's kings did to Israel's priests. Their agenda differs considerably from ours. Yet their efforts to keep order, peace, and stability throughout the world create the conditions in which we render our priestly service and offer our priestly praise. They shape the context in which we sing our songs and submit our testimony to Christ's lordship.

Christ has not placed this world under the church's feet. We have not been commissioned to tell the powers what to do or how to think. Nor has Christ made us their servants such that we might obey them when that would contravene God's will for us in Christ. Like us, their interests are best served by confessing and aligning their lives with Christ's lordship. Jesus offers his kingdom to them as to us, as a gift. So we meet them where they are and address them at their level of receptivity to God's gift. When they eagerly hear our ideas, we praise God for their receptivity and testify to what God has done. When they seek to sing along with us, we teach them the songs of the redeemed. When they revile us, persecute us, and try to silence our voices, we praise God that we've been counted worthy of sharing in Christ's sufferings. When they brush us aside or ignore us, we implore God to soften their hearts as we steadfastly sing his praises. Our faith requires neither the interest nor acceptance of all people and powers. We will sing the Lord's praises all the more when the world shuts its ears to our songs.

IMPLICATIONS FOR THE CHURCH

Though a posture of praise should encompass our entire lives, here I explore how it might inform our stance toward the unbelieving world. What does it mean to praise God in our neighborhood, workplace, public square, or state capital? The prophetic, kingly, and servant churches inhabit these spaces in diverse ways—sometimes criticizing, sometimes ruling, sometimes serving wherever needed. These approaches have yielded mixed results historically, depending on the world's receptivity. In today's context, criticizing often leads to resentment. People who don't share our standards object when we impose our convictions upon them. In today's context, ruling leads to over-reach. Neither God nor our unbelieving neighbors have asked believers to exercise oversight in light of our faith. Doing so makes us look controlling. In today's context, Christian service is often coopted by various powers and principalities. Sincere kingdom efforts are made to serve worldly ambitions, whether political or financial. This, in turn, plays into the hands of worldly factionalism, and our witness to God's kingdom can be lost.

I've been arguing that the priestly posture remains the most promising and least explored posture for reframing church-world relations. As priestly exiles, we engage the world as guests on their turf. We don't presume to be in charge but are uniquely positioned to serve in ways that our disentanglement allows. As hospitable priests, we take risks and reach out to those whom society deems unfit or unworthy. As priestly stewards of Christ's sacrifice, we maintain a rugged commitment to the sanctity of all life. We, therefore, seek the good of all parties, especially those most likely to be ignored or dismissed. As priestly witnesses, our testimony flows from the positive example we live out in our own lives. We act before we expect others to act. We live lives worth imitating, which points others to God's kingdom. *What* we might say and *how* we might say it remain to be discussed. Here I address four aspects of priestly speech to the world that flow from a heart of praise.

Speaking Freely

When Peter and John preached Jesus in Jerusalem during the early days of the church, the establishment tried to shut them down. Having no legal grounds, they attempted to silence the apostles, ordering them not to teach in Jesus's name. Peter and John promptly replied, "Whether it is right in God's sight to listen to you rather than to God, you must judge; for we cannot keep from speaking about what we have seen and heard" (Acts 4:19–20). The leaders didn't take the hint. Nor did the apostles acquiesce. They kept preaching Jesus and causing trouble. The High Priest (now functioning as an agent of Roman peace) rebuked them, saying, "We gave you strict orders not to teach in this name" (Acts 5:28). Peter and the apostles responded more directly this time:

> We must obey God rather than any human authority. The God of our ancestors raised up Jesus, whom you had killed by hanging him on a

tree. God exalted him at his right hand as Leader and Savior that he might give repentance to Israel and forgiveness of sins. And we are witnesses to these things, and so is the Holy Spirit whom God has given to those who obey him. (Acts 5:29–32)

The apostles refused to be silenced. How could they heed the words of men, when God raised Jesus from the dead and seated him on high? Praise overflowed from every fiber of their being. Since we have received the same Spirit who testified to these things, we too must speak freely of what God has done in Jesus. We, too, must confess Jesus as the one whom God placed by his side in heavenly places. Mere men cannot silence Christ's lordship. The Spirit won't allow it.

The notion of an exalted Lord threatens authorities still today. They want no part in a heavenly ruler whose authority might place limits on their own. They have no room for a version of truth that disagrees with their agenda or pits them against constituents who keep them in power. Yet God has given us something to say, so we freely say it regardless of what the authorities want, or what our boss, family, and church leaders desire. Consider the following representative instances when God's people should feel free to speak from a posture of praise:

- When anyone pressures us to participate in activities that violate our convictions about Christ's lordship and its claim on our lives.
- When our commitment to Christ's lordship adds something unique and important to wider public conversations.
- When anyone undermines the sanctity of life in what they say, what they do, or how they treat others (this pertains directly to our stewardship of Christ's sacrifice).
- When people profane God's name in word or deed.
- When governing authorities neglect their mandate to reward the good and punish the evil.
- When commanders overstep the bounds of their authority by using the sword to expand their territory, accumulate wealth, achieve fame, create a utopia, or give the appearance of being productive— God only authorized their use of the sword to curb evil.
- When people of influence speak as if they were divine or strive to wield absolute authority without accountability.

- When anyone works to create conditions in which Christ's church cannot carry out our mandate to proclaim God's word of truth.
- When God's Spirit gives us something concrete to say.
- When people ask us to give an account of our hope.

This list serves only as a beginning. However, we must remember that our freedom to speak does not provide a blank check to say whatever we want, to whomever we want, however we want. Our kingdom mandate constrains our speech in important ways. The next three aspects of priestly praise spell out some of those constraints.

Speaking Truthfully

During Pilate's interrogation, Jesus didn't say much. Yet what he told Pilate speaks to a key component of Christian speech to the powers: "You would have no power over me unless it had been given you from above; therefore the one who handed me over to you is guilty of a greater sin" (John 19:11). On the one hand, Jesus reminds the Roman prefect of his place in the divine pecking order. Pilate talks like a man who believes he holds the power of life and death in his hands: "Do you not know that I have power to release you, and power to crucify you?" (John 19:10). To a certain extent, he is right. Pilate makes the final call that leads people like Jesus to Golgotha and people like Barabbas to freedom. Yet Jesus delivers Pilate from his delusions of grandeur. First, he reminds Pilate that any authority he wields derives from God. He will therefore answer to God for all lives that he takes. Second, Jesus informs Pilate that he's not even as responsible for Jesus's life as he thinks. The High Priest and his court of power hungry leaders conspired to have Jesus killed. Pilate is just a pawn.

Jesus speaks to Pilate on his own terms and in the context of his own world. He also addresses Pilate at his point of need. Jesus declares God's reign over rulers and its implications for Pilate's situation. Jesus speaks from a posture of praise. He speaks truth to people where they are, which derives from the truth of God's reign over all the earth. Pilate probably didn't appreciate that truth. It meant he was accountable to a power outside the Roman system that he had managed to navigate successfully. No wonder he tried to make Jesus go away. No wonder he felt compelled to wash his bloodstained hands. Even his wife claims to have received a word from on high.[25] Pilate would surely have to answer for this life, which was not his to take.

We, too, must speak truthfully to the powers of this world. But the truth we speak, as believers, should derive from the gospel of God's kingship and Jesus's lordship. This truth the psalmists continually offered up in praise. Jesus spoke this truth to Pilate and the apostles spoke it to Jewish authorities. The Spirit bears witness to this gospel truth. No other truth boasts that kind of backing.

On the contrary, believers are *not* free, divinely authorized, and Spirit empowered to give Christianized takes on anything and everything. Jesus and his witnesses did not merely parrot or echo what unbelievers were already saying. They did not speak with divine authority about the latest in Roman court intrigue. They didn't offer commentary on the new road systems or various border skirmishes. They proclaimed the relevance of Christ's lordship to specific situations they encountered in the course of seeking first God's kingdom mission.

We must not speak a message in Jesus's name that differs from Christ's kingdom and lordship. To do so takes his name in vain and risks profaning it for non-kingdom causes. The lordship of Jesus doesn't tell us who should be president or who makes a good supreme court justice. It doesn't tell us how unbelievers should regulate mind-altering substances or how pagans should approach marriage. It doesn't tell us how the world should manage an unwieldy viral pandemic that we all know little about. The lordship of Jesus speaks directly to the dignity of all oppressed people everywhere, but it falls short of explaining the best legislative paths to true equality in a particular country with a complex history. Christians should not hesitate to speak clearly and directly about what Jesus's lordship means for a wide variety of issues and situations, but they should speak cautiously about worldly strategies for addressing them. The Spirit in us bears witness to what God has done in Christ, not what those outside of Christ might do in each and every circumstance. The following cases exemplify what truthful Christian speech might sound like regarding highly contested public issues:

---

25. Matt 27:19.

- When the world wants to abort babies, we speak the truth that God exercises exclusive authority over all life, that no human has the right to take it, and that Christians gladly offer generous hospitality to women who can't imagine bringing their baby to full term, to mothers who lack resources to care for their child postpartum, and to babies whose mothers are unable to care for them for whatever reason.[26]

- When nations struggle with the best way to manage their borders, we speak the truth that all territories belong to God, that God cares deeply for aliens and refugees, that God holds all people and powers accountable for how they treat those who come to them in need, and that God's alien people eagerly open up their homes, wallets, schedules, and sanctuaries to help assimilate those who are struggling to make a new start in alien territory.

- When societies struggle to eradicate racism in their midst, we speak the truth that all humans are made in God's image, that all people must be treated with equal dignity, that God judges those who discriminate against others, that all powers that perpetuate such discrimination will be brought low, that Christ has broken down the wall that separates all people, and that his people represent a new humanity—among whom there is neither male nor female, slave nor free, Jew nor Gentile, black nor white, citizen or alien, rich nor poor—where we value each person, prioritize each person's needs, equip each person to serve the common good, forgive each person their sins, and strive to exemplify kingdom equality in all aspects of our lives together.

In each case, we exalt our Lord who wants what is best for all people and holds accountable those who do harm. We clearly state what God has revealed to be right and wrong. And we draw attention to the kingdom community where abundant life may be experienced now—even amid a wider world that continues to manifest and perpetuate the friction and fragmentation that sin begets. In each case, we offer good news of a real-life alternative vision and experience. We don't pretend we know how to fix the complex, deeply

---

26. For some compelling stories of how believers have come alongside mothers contemplating abortion, see Brittany Smith and Natasha Smith, *Unplanned Grace: A Compassionate Conversation on Life and Choice* (Colorado Springs: David C. Cook, 2021).

entrenched, and sometimes intractably corrupt structures behind this world's problems. But we strive to diagnose them forthrightly, voice the need for change, and alert all people to the lasting change that has already begun in Christ. Anything less falls short of our calling; anything more lies beyond it and cannot invoke the same divine backing.

Speaking Hopefully

Speaking freely and truthfully addresses the *when* and the *what* of priestly speech to the world. The next two points address the *how*, without which the *what* is usually compromised. When Paul found an audience before the Roman Procurator, Festus, and King Agrippa, he proclaimed Jesus as the one who forgives our sins and whom God raised from the dead. Paul related how God spoke to him from heaven to correct his course. He even expressed his desire that his interrogators might see the light as well. The back-and-forth exchange that ensued is somewhat humorous. The apostle begins,

> "King Agrippa, do you believe the prophets? I know that you believe."
> Agrippa said to Paul, "Are you so quickly persuading me to become a Christian?" Paul replied, "Whether quickly or not, I pray to God that not only you but also all who are listening to me today might become such as I am—except for these chains." (Acts 26:27–29)

Paul held nothing back, and he proclaimed his message with confidence. He must have sensed during his testimony that the king was beginning to soften. Seizing the moment, he appealed to the Spirit's work in Agrippa's heart: "I know that you believe." It reminds me of *Star Wars: Return of the Jedi*, when Luke appeals to Darth Vader, "I know there is good in you." Of course, the king quickly dismissed Paul, but Paul doesn't back down. Instead, he affirms his hope and prayer that not only Agrippa but everyone in attendance might join the way of Jesus—though perhaps without the annoyance of being thrown in jail.

Jesus, Peter, and John displayed this same boldness. The priestly psalmists also exhibited this boldness as they professed Israel's God as king in the face of human rulers who aspired for absolute sway, systematically pushed Torah aside, and domesticated the priests. We pick up no hint of fear or anger in any of these testimonies. God's people truly believe in his sovereign rule over world history. They know with certainty that mere human authorities pale in comparison to

God's power and ultimate significance. Christ advocates at God's right hand for his followers and through him they, too, possess heavenly standing. In Paul's words, "God, who is rich in mercy, out of the great love with which he loved us even when we were dead through our trespasses, made us alive together with Christ—by grace you have been saved—and raised us up with him and seated us with him in the heavenly places in Christ Jesus" (Eph 2:4–6).

Those seated with Christ, the exalted Lord, have no reason to fear governing authorities. We have no reason to be insecure about our message to them. We speak as hopeful people. We represent a kingdom that is firmly established and cannot be shaken. We bring a message of good news regardless of whether people accept it. Even when they refuse to align with God's kingdom and purposes, our mission has not failed. God still reigns on high. He raises up rulers and brings them low. Should a particular administration fail to take our mandate seriously, God has myriad options for accomplishing his will, nonetheless.

As believers, we mourn the injustices and loss of life that takes place under the watch of fallen powers. Our confidence in God's victory and security in our inheritance does not make us cold to the suffering of others, but it guards us from despair. Nor does it tempt us to forsake our calling to seek some other, presumably more effective way to make people change. God has already revealed his most effective way. We remain radically devoted to God's way in seasons of effectiveness and seasons of frustration. We speak as those with hope because we have faith. Echoing the prophet Habakkuk, we praise

> Though the fig tree does not blossom,
>   and no fruit is on the vines;
> though the produce of the olive fails
>   and the fields yield no food;
> though the flock is cut off from the fold
>   and there is no herd in the stalls,
> yet I will rejoice in the LORD;
>   I will exult in the God of my salvation.
> GOD, the Lord, is my strength;
>   he makes my feet like the feet of a deer,
> and makes me tread upon the heights. (Hab 3:17–19)

When we testify to the world concerning the lordship of Christ, people should occasionally scoff and ask us, "Do you think you've actually made a believer out of me?" Our confident optimism in the power of God's Spirit at work should energize our testimony. People should not feel like we are begging them to hear us out. Our eyes should beam with hope as we praise God in their hearing. Our comfortable, confident resolve should have them scratching their heads, wondering if we might be onto something after all.

Speaking hopefully is not a five-step process. It is a disposition that we catch and it flows from a life lived in Christ and in his Spirit. When we constantly saddle ourselves with worldly cares and concerns, we lose some of that hope. We trade the light burden of Christ for the heavy burden of possessions and control. When we seek first God's kingdom—prioritizing kingdom witness with our time, energy, and resources—we experience kingdom power and presence. When we calibrate our faith with regular prayer, Scripture reading, fellowship, and outreach, the hope of Christ infuses our being. As participants in God's goodness, we radiate that goodness in word and deed. When we crowd out the kingdom by prioritizing anything else, praise degenerates into complaint, despair replaces hope, and we have little to offer that the world doesn't already have.

Speaking Graciously

> In that region there were shepherds living in the fields, keeping watch over their flock by night. Then an angel of the Lord stood before them, and the glory of the Lord shone around them, and they were terrified. But the angel said to them, "Do not be afraid; for see—I am bringing you good news of great joy for all the people: to you is born this day in the city of David a Savior, who is the Messiah, the Lord." (Luke 2:8–11)

This passage is perhaps too familiar to us, with the repeated exposure it gets each Christmas season. Perhaps you even skimmed past it before reading this. But the coming of Jesus as Savior, Messiah, and Lord brings "good news of great joy *for all the people*." Jesus's incarnation serves as good news *for all* because it means peace on earth, at last. It is *good* news because God gave Jesus as a gift to the whole world. His kingdom brings an end to wars and rumors of wars, which means peace and prosperity for all people.

We sometimes remind Christians who live sluggishly in their faith that Jesus is not just their Savior, but also their Lord. By this, we often mean that they should take obedience to Christ more seriously. When we do that, however, we risk drawing upon worldly notions of lordship that strike fear into people. You wouldn't want your lord to be angry, so you better clean up your act. But the lordship of Jesus brings good news. He rules as the most benevolent lord. More than any king, he wants what is best for his people and all people. He comes as a servant king who invites all people into his kingdom.

We, indeed, receive Jesus's benevolent reign as good news. It means the end of ruthless dictators. It spells the end of slavery, exploitation, and fear. Oppression plays no part in his reign. Unbelievers should welcome the good news that the wars and pestilence that plague this world will end decisively. We are not waiting for a comet to come along and wipe out all life. World history moves in a specific direction, and we look forward to the best possible outcome.

Christ's reign also rings as good news for people in power. They saddle themselves with the burden that if they don't get something done for the good of this world, then it's not going to happen. They resort to threats and manipulation to get everyone on board because they're not sure they can pull it off without total support. Because they never win such support, they live in constant fear and conflict with those who stand in their way. It is good news that the future of world history does not depend on them. Their best efforts at world management lack ultimate significance. What a relief that God reigns on high, that he looks after the good of his creation, and that he rewards those who seek his face.

In two places, the apostle Paul concisely spells out the gift nature of our faith: "For the wages of sin is death, but the free gift of God is eternal life in Christ Jesus our Lord" (Rom 6:23) and "For by grace you have been saved through faith, and this is not your own doing; it is the gift of God" (Eph 2:8). We must never forget that God's people serve as nothing more and nothing less than gift bearers on God's behalf. We bear this gift in our lives, in our fellowship with one another, and in our proclamation to the world. The apostle John says it this way: "For God so loved the world that he gave his only Son, so that everyone who believes in him may not perish but may have eternal life. Indeed, God did not send the Son into the world to condemn the world, but in order that the world might be saved through him" (John 3:16–17).

Anything we say to the world must flow from the gift we have to offer. Jesus did not enter this world to condemn it, and he certainly did not send us into the world as stewards of condemnation. The world hears our message as we praise God. See what God has done in Jesus! See what his cross has accomplished. See how he graciously invites us all into it! We need not live at odds with God anymore. We were once estranged from God, but in Christ God has drawn us near.

I wonder what it might look like for us to frame all our discourse with the world in terms of God's gracious gift. I imagine it's possible, and I suspect it would revolutionize the church's witness for the good. Here I offer a few suggestions as to what it could look like:

- Instead of saying, "You can't legalize gay marriage! Homosexuality is an abomination to God, and encouraging people to engage in that practice will corrupt our children and tear apart civilization as we know it!" we could say, "This is such a complicated issue. We all have different reasons for thinking the way we do about sex and marriage. Without a common faith to unite us, it seems that wide-spread consensus is impossible. One thing we can all agree on is that God loves all people and gives them freedom to make choices, even those that go against his will. How can we create space for people of different convictions to coexist peacefully and avoid constant discrimination without retooling our education system so as to indoctrinate children into hotly contested positions on this topic?"
- Instead of saying, "You can't fight that war! Those are real people on the other side and we will protest, riot, and impugn your name in every form of media at our disposal until you withdraw!" we say, "Jesus is Lord over all nations, each one is precious to him, and he calls for peace. What kinds of changes will be necessary for you to feel safe and how might we mediate between opposing parties to work quickly toward peace? We pray fervently for peace. What do you recommend we focus on? What needs to happen before you will feel comfortable declaring a ceasefire? What steps are being taken to safeguard civilians on the other side? What might we do to offset unintended harm inflicted to lives, homes, and communities as collateral damage? Some of our people refuse to fight wars on grounds of faith; we implore you to honor their objections and provide peaceful alternatives should a draft ever be deemed necessary."
- Instead of saying, "You can't mandate vaccines! We demand freedom of choice! You just want to control our bodies, line the

pockets of big pharma, and score political points with your base," we say, "We sympathize with the government's dilemma. They are trying to control something that is beyond human control and to keep safe as many people as possible. But Jesus is the Lord of life and government is not. At their best, governments can only apply blanket solutions that cover the majority, whereas health needs vary significantly from person to person and risk levels vary from region to region. Would you consider extending the same freedom citizens are afforded to practice diverse religions and to embrace risky lifestyles to those who wish to refrain from preventative medicine they believe does more harm than good? We recognize the risks of giving freedom in this area, as well as the risks of striving to control what cannot be controlled. We also recognize the authority God gives governments, and we don't expect they will always make decisions we affirm. Still, we pray that God grants them supernatural wisdom, and we will submit to their decisions to the extent that they function within God's will. We will peacefully disobey when they violate God's will, and we are prepared to face the consequences peaceably whatever those may be. We confess that we are not experts in pandemics either. So when new and reliable evidence clarifies what is best for the common good, we will gladly change our practice accordingly."

These suggestions, of course, oversimplify extremely complex issues. I offer them as samples of how believers from different vantage points might advocate them graciously. I am trying to convey the right tone rather than a complete answer or even the right answer. In practice, each conversation should be tailored to the dialog partner and the specific situation. Each conversation should be conducted in the spirit of freedom, hope, truth, and grace. When we engage the world on such terms, our testimony rises to God as a fragrant offering of praise.

These responses are infused with grace insofar as they give the benefit of the doubt to their conversation partner, display integrity with humility in their convictions, and express hope in a positive resolution. These responses recognize that Christians do not govern. Christians offer to be part of the solution in ways consistent with their faith. And they accept the outcome peaceably one way or another. At the same time, they never waver on God's ultimate authority, even as they acknowledge the important responsibility he gives public officials.

These grace-filled conversations represent those that exiles are best suited to carry on. They reveal a posture of strength from a position of lowliness. They strike a tone similar to that of Daniel and his friends when they spoke with foreign rulers during Babylonian exile. They refused to eat food that would compromise their Jewish identity, so their overseer pressured them. Consider Daniel's gracious response: "Please test your servants for ten days. Let us be given vegetables to eat and water to drink. You can then compare our appearance with the appearance of the young men who eat the royal rations, and deal with your servants according to what you observe" (Dan 1:12–13). Likewise, when asked to account for why they wouldn't pay homage to a political-religious monument, Daniel's friends answered, "O Nebuchadnezzar, we have no need to present a defense to you in this matter. If our God whom we serve is able to deliver us from the furnace of blazing fire and out of your hand, O king, let him deliver us. But if not, be it known to you, O king, that we will not serve your gods and we will not worship the golden statue that you have set up" (Dan 3:16–18). In both cases, God honored his people's grace-laced resistance. After the statue incident, Nebuchadnezzar changed course and paid homage to Israel's God, saying,

> Blessed be the God of Shadrach, Meshach, and Abednego, who has sent his angel and delivered his servants who trusted in him. They disobeyed the king's command and yielded up their bodies rather than serve and worship any god except their own God. Therefore I make a decree: Any people, nation, or language that utters blasphemy against the God of Shadrach, Meshach, and Abednego shall be torn limb from limb, and their houses laid in ruins; for there is no other god who is able to deliver in this way. (Dan 3:28–29)

A posture of praise holds great power and great promise. Yet such a posture does not come naturally to us. We often settle for lesser aims that fall short of giving God glory. We focus instead on getting our way, proving we are right, preserving our way of life, staying out of trouble, or maintaining our sense of control. In such instances, even when we win, we still end up losing. We lose respect when we fight hard and win a battle that only ends up later being discredited. We lose momentum when we take strong stands on issues where Christians themselves are divided and church unity takes a hit. Our witness to believers takes a hit along with our unity. We lose kingdom ground when we champion a political cause that ends up hurting a significant number of unbelievers. Defeated unbelievers end up resenting God and the church for our interference.

Could it be that God created his people as a lowly people without access to worldly power precisely because he wanted us to offer his gift of salvation in ways that are *not* alienating? Could God want his people to be inviting to the lost and confused people he wishes to save? When we make sincere efforts to produce positive wide-scale societal change in one fell swoop—whether through an election, piece of legislation, or Supreme Court nominee—we wield a form of power that undermines our ability to make the small-scale changes of heart that remain central to God's chosen strategy for advancing his kingdom in this world. Israel and the church both tried their hands at wielding top-down worldly power to accomplish kingdom ends. Perhaps it's time we lift our voice in priestly praise instead.

Conclusion

A DIFFERENT KIND OF PRIEST

God's word is living and active and sharper than a double-edged sword (Heb 4:12). The author of Hebrews speaks powerfully to a congregation in turmoil. They had doubts about their faith. They were plagued by guilty consciences. They thought Jesus wasn't enough. Some stopped gathering altogether. They stood on the brink of apostasy. They couldn't get over their sin problem. The old covenant priesthood and sacrificial system provided time-tested mechanisms for dealing with human failings, but the new covenant appeared to be soft on sin. It has no priest, no temple, and no sacrifices. They readily affirmed that Jesus fulfilled the Messianic mission of gathering the Israelites, forgiving the sins that scattered them, and inaugurating God's kingdom. But how does that help with the ongoing sins of Christians? The waters of baptism washed away their old sins, but what about their new ones? The son of David may have come, but where's the son of Aaron? Jesus was the king they were waiting for, but where was the priest they needed?

The book of Hebrews argues both elegantly and persuasively that even though Jesus was not from the line of Levi, God still ordained him as priest.[27] Jesus hails from the line of Melchizedek, who preceded Levi and served the priestly needs of father Abraham. As Levi's lineage serviced the old covenant, Melchizedek's heir services the new covenant. The blood of animals once covered Israel's sins, year after year. The blood of Jesus now atones for all the world's sins, once for all time. Jesus was not the priest the Israelites were waiting for, but he was the priest they needed.

Many Christians today harbor doubts. Churches wallow in turmoil. We have made a mess of our witness and the world has noticed. Previously well-established believers have deconstructed their faith and remain unsure where

---

27. Heb 5–7.

to turn next. Few have a problem with Jesus. They appreciate what he stood for; he has always inspired them. But the church of their experience cannot be what Jesus intended. Meddling in worldly politics. Propping up capitalism. Legislating morality. Judging unbelievers. Ignoring community health concerns. Rejecting modern science. Scorning public education. Fighting among themselves. Perpetuating racism. Subjugating women. Protecting pedophiles. Disrespecting law enforcement. Shaming gays. Celebritizing pastors. Parroting pop culture. Hopping on bandwagons. Contributing little of significance to wider society.

So much of the damage Christians have inflicted stems from faulty visions of the church's mandate. Those flawed visions are grounded in confused notions of the church's place in this world. *Kingly churches* insinuate themselves into positions of top-down power and influence in hopes of steering society in a kingdom-like direction. Like Gentile rulers of old, they exercise authority over others that they might serve as society's divinely appointed benefactors. They possess good motives and they foster noble ideals, but the specter of Christendom still haunts their best efforts.

Servant churches tire of all the negative press. They hope to engender goodwill by identifying problem areas where society wants help and finding practical ways to be part of the solution. Insofar as they render such service and their efforts are well-received, these churches do considerable good. Yet prioritizing the world's needs leads many to accept the world's misdiagnoses of their problems. The word of God stands in judgment upon both the oppressive forces that create such needs and the fallen structures that presume to know the problem yet routinely botch the solution.

Prophetic churches don't hesitate to bring a divine word. They frequently tap into existing social unrest by publicly decrying what outspoken activists already decry—only, in Christian language. Their prophetic voice gets lost in the preexisting chorus they seem to have joined. Those activists whose causes they champion embrace them as allies. Those they criticize write them off as false prophets serving as ventriloquist dummies for the other side. In both instances, people seldom hear a fresh word from the Lord.

Priestly churches strive to stay above the fray. They recognize that this world has problems and that God addresses these problems in two distinct ways. He calls churches to focus on spiritual needs and worldly structures to care for social needs. When the church succeeds at inner transformation, outward transformation naturally follows—and worldly structures will have less problems to solve. Yet this tidy division of responsibilities doesn't square well with Torah or the Sermon on the Mount. Israel and the church's mandates have always encompassed spiritual and social, inward and outward concerns. Both the brokenness of this world and the healing words of Scripture call for a different kind of priestly church.

PRIESTLY CHURCH REVISITED

The priestly model checks many boxes from a biblical perspective. Both the Old and the New Testament apply the priestly model to God's people in prominent places with significant weight. It's a shame when Christians strip the priestly heritage of its sociopolitical significance. This happens most often when people reduce priestly service to the responsibility of Aaron's sons, which revolved around the tabernacle or temple. I have argued at length that when we expand our vision to include all Levites scattered throughout Israel's tribes, a fuller picture emerges that addresses the priestly model's chief weaknesses. From this vantage point, I highlighted five aspects of priestly life that pertained both to the wider people of Israel *and* the church of Jesus Christ. Taken together, they form a rich priestly model for the church that goes a long way to clarify its witness to the world.

The Levites played a special role in ancient Israel. They exemplified what it means to be God's set-apart servants, mediators, heralds, witnesses, and lyricists. In calling Israel a nation of priests, Scripture reminds us that the Levites were not the only exemplary people in Palestine. To the extent that all the people of Israel lived lightly in their own land, extended risky hospitality to others, honored God's exclusive claim on life, ordered their lives around Torah, and elevated the King of kings as Lord of all; they performed their own priestly role and serve as powerful witnesses to both the church and the world.

This revised priestly model does not derive from any particular church tradition and represents no particular Christian niche. It draws from the Old and New Testaments, which all churches hold in common. The model represents neither high church nor low church, Catholic nor Protestant, Western nor Eastern, progressive nor evangelical. It thus possesses great potential to unite believers from a wide variety of Christian heritages. It affirms and includes the best insights of the kingly, servant, prophetic, and traditional priestly models. We desperately need such unity in our divided times.

WELCOME *BACK* TO THE PRIESTLY CHURCH

God uses world powers to promote order and keep evil from wreaking too much havoc in this world. At their best, they reward the good and punish wickedness. At their worst, they presume to hold the power of life and death and aspire to control the direction of world history. Sometimes they aim to impose their will upon all; other times they strive to engineer some sort of utopia. Yet Jesus is Lord of world history and God alone reserves the right to give and take life. As Creator, only God knows what makes for human flourishing and only he can bring about a new and glorious kingdom. He has not appointed territorial powers to represent this kingdom; he has appointed his trans-territorial priestly people to this task.

God changed the course of world history by sending Jesus to inaugurate his kingdom on earth. Our priestly calling entails representing that kingdom to the whole world and inviting all people to share in it. The Scriptures issue this priestly mandate in numerous passages at pivotal moments, including Exodus 19:5–6; Isaiah 61:6; Romans 12:1–2; 1 Peter 2:4–5, 9; and Revelation 1:5–6; 5:9–10. Though this mandate determines all aspects of our lives, five priestly aspects convey the basic gist:

- Priestly Residence: We live as exiles scattered throughout creation, unattached to the fading structures of this world so we can serve the world in unique ways that only unattached people can.
- Priestly Hospitality: We strive to be safe havens in this world, offering risky hospitality to all people. Our disentanglement from governing structures makes us uniquely impartial and thus able to welcome and work for the peace of all people.
- Priestly Stewardship: We proclaim Jesus Christ as the sacrifice to end all sacrifices who won eternal peace through the cross. We steward his sacrifice by honoring all life, laying down our lives for others, and proclaiming Christ's sole jurisdiction over all life.
- Priestly Witness: We confess Jesus as creator and redeemer of this world. He uniquely knows how to promote the flourishing of all creation in anticipation of new creation. He ordained us to bear witness to his intentions for this world in all that we say and do.
- Priestly Praise: We praise God for making us foretastes of his new creation and using us to welcome the whole world into it. We receive

this life as a precious gift and so we extend it to others with an attitude of praise in freedom, truth, hope, and grace.

As God's holy people, God has set us apart from the world. But like Israel's priests, we are only set apart *from* the world so we might exist *for* the world. Our status as exiles and aliens sometimes feels like a liability. But we trust God that priestly disentanglement from worldly methods of change and control perfectly positions us to serve this world in ways that only we can. For the world's sake, we embrace, display, and proclaim God's kingdom as God's gift to the world through Christ.

We are a royal priesthood, a holy nation, God's own people, proclaiming the mighty acts of him who called us out of darkness into his marvelous light!

Appendix 1

New Testament Passages
Related to Peace

1. Christians must not kill, remain angry, or name call (Matt 5:21–22; Rom 13:8–10; Eph 4:31; Col 3:8; 1 Tim 2:8; Jas 1:19–20; 4:1–4; 1 Pet 2:1)
2. Christians must love their enemies (Matt 5:44; Luke 6:35; Rom 12:20)
3. Christian love is distinct from non-Christian love precisely in that we love our enemies (Matt 5:44–48; Luke 6:32–36)
4. Christians must overcome evil with good (Rom 12:21)
5. Christians must not repay evil with evil (Rom 12:17; 1 Thess 5:15; 1 Pet 3:9)
6. Christians must not repay abuse with abuse (1 Pet 2:23; 3:9)
7. Christians must never take revenge and must leave it to God (Rom 12:19; Jas 4:12; 1 Pet 2:23; cf., 2 Thess 1:4–9 & Heb 10:30)
8. Christians are called to a life of suffering/persecution/trials and must bear under them gladly to the point of death (Matt 5:10–12; 10:23; 12:21; 24:9; Mark 8:31–38; 10:29–30; 13:11; Luke 9:22–26; 21:12–19; John 15:20; Rom 5:3–4; 8:17–18; 8:35–39; 1 Cor 4:12; 2 Cor 1:5–11; 4:7–11; 12:9–10; Phil 1:29–30; 3:10; Col 1:34; 1 Thess 1:6; 2:14; 3:3; 2 Thess 1:4–9; 2 Tim 1:8; 3:12; 4:5; Heb 2:9–10; 10:32–39; Jas 1:2–4; 1:12; 1 Pet 1:6–7; 2:18–25; 3:13–18; 4:1–2; 4:12–19; 5:6–10; Rev 1:9; 2:10–11)
9. Christians must bless those who curse us (Luke 6:28; Rom 12:14; 1 Cor 4:12; 1 Pet 3:9)
10. Christians must pray for those who persecute us (Matt 5:44; Luke 6:28)

11. Christians must do good to those who hate us (Luke 6:27, 35; 1 Cor 4:12–13)

12. Christians must do to others as we would have them do to us (Matt 7:12; Luke 6:31)

13. Christians must give to those who are trying to take from us, rather than resist (Matt 5:39–42; Luke 6:29–30; Rom 12:20; Heb 10:34)

14. Christians must be merciful as God is merciful (Matt 5:7; 23:23; Luke 6:36; 10:36–37; Jas 2:13; 3:17; Jude 1:20–23)

15. Christians must not judge nor condemn (Matt 7:1–6; Luke 6:37; John 7:24; Rom 2:1–6; 14:1–13; 1 Cor 4:4; 5:12–13; Jas 2:13; 4:11–12)

16. Christians must forgive (Matt 6:12–15; 18:21–35; Mark 11:25–26; Luke 6:37; 11:4; 17:3–4; John 20:22–23; Eph 4:32; Col 3:13; Jas 5:14–16)

17. Christians are involved in a battle for a kingdom, but we do not use worldly weapons (Matt 10:34–39 [cf. Luke 12:51–53]; 26:52; John 18:36; 2 Cor 10:3–6; Eph 6:10–17)

18. Christians must live peaceably with all (Matt 5:9; Mark 9:50; Acts 10:34–36; Rom 12:18; 14:17–19; 1 Cor 7:15; Gal 5:22; Eph 2:13–22; 6:15; Col 1:19–20; 1 Thess 5:13; 2 Tim 2:22; Titus 3:1–7; Heb 12:14; Jas 3:17–18; 1 Pet 3:10–12; 2 Pet 3:14)

19. Christians are called to reconciliation (Matt 5:23–26; 18:15–20; 2 Cor 5:16–19; Eph 2:13–16)

20. Christians are not to fear for our lives, futures, or possessions (Matt 10:28–31; Luke 1:68–75; 4:4–7; 12:4–7; 12:31–34; John 14:27; Rom 8:15; Heb 2:14–15; 13:5–6; 1 Pet 3:6; 3:14; 1 John 4:18; Rev 2:10)

Appendix 2
Distinguishing Marks of a Kingdom Displaying Church

1. Places God's Kingdom above all else (Matt 6:33; 13:44–46; Mark 9:47–48; Luke 12:30–31; 18:28–30)
2. Shows equality on multiple levels: gender, race, age, heritage, social/economic status, and religious status (1 Cor 12:12–13; 2 Cor 5:16–17; Gal 3:26–29; Eph 2:11–22; Col 3:9–11)
3. Unifies through diversity (John 17:20–24; 1 Cor 1:10; 12:12–27; Eph 4:1–6, 14–16)
4. Lives by love: fellow believers (John 13:34–35; 1 Pet 1:22; 2:17; 4:8), enemies (Matt 5:43–48), and outcasts (Matt 25:31–46)
5. Accepts persecution and suffering (Acts 14:22; Rom 5:3–5; Jas 1:2–4; 1 Pet 3:13–14; 4:12–16)
6. Forgives and reconciles at all levels (Matt 6:14–15; 18:15–35; John 20:22–23; 2 Cor 5:18–19)
7. Confuses those not in tune with God's Spirit (Mark 4:11–20; 1 Cor 1:18–25; 2:6–16)
8. Follows the Spirit's leading (John 16:13–15; Rom 8:13–14; 1 Cor 2:10–16; Gal 5:25)
9. Embodies cross-shaped wisdom (Mark 8:34–35; 1 Cor 1:17–2:16; Jas 3:13–18)
10. Exhibits sincere, diligent, fruit-bearing faith (Matt 5:20; 13:18–23; 21:33–44; 25:1–30; Luke 9:62)
11. Values children and childlikeness (Matt 18:1–5; 19:13–14; Mark 10:13–16; Luke 18:15–17)
12. Assimilates the poor more easily than the wealthy (Matt 19:23–24; Luke 6:20–21; Jas 2:5)

13. Welcomes the undeserving and unexpected (Matt 20:1–16; 21:28–32; 22:2–14)

14. Flees from and repents of immorality (1 Cor 5:1–5; 6:18–20; 2 Cor 6:14–18; Gal 5:16–21; Eph 5:5; 1 Pet 2:9–12; 4:1–3)

15. Grows in ways only God understands (Mark 4:26–29; Luke 17:20–21; Col 2:18–19)

16. Cultivates Christ-like spirituality (Rom 8:9–17; Gal 5:22–26)

17. Expresses concern for the marginalized of society (Matt 25:31–46; Luke 4:18–21; Jas 1:27)

18. Assumes a humble servant posture (Matt 5:3; 18:1–4; 20:20–28; Mark 9:33–35; John 13:1–17)

19. Attracts frauds as well as genuine converts (Matt 13:24–30, 47–50; 1 Cor 11:19)

20. Esteems small, unimpressive beginnings (Matt 13:31–32; 1 Cor 1:26–31)

21. Infiltrates the world (Luke 13:21)

22. Seeks peace even when it hurts (Matt 5:38–48; Rom 12:17–21; 1 Cor 6:7; 1 Pet 2:18–25; 3:9–17; Rev 2:9–10; 7:9–17)

23. Makes Christ-like disciples (John 13:12–17; Rom 8:28–30; 1 Cor 11:1; 2 Cor 3:18; 1 Pet 2:21–25; 1 John 4:17)

24. Hopes in a bodily resurrection (1 Cor 15:12–23), eternal life (Gal 6:7–10), restoration of earth (Rom 8:18–25; Rev 21), judgment on powers and personalities counter to God's kingdom (1 Cor 15:24–28; Col 2:15)

25. Accesses God's power through prayer (Matt 21:18–22; Luke 11:9–13; Jas 5:13–20)

Bibliography

Arnold, Johann Christoph. *Why Forgive?* Maryknoll, NY: Orbis Books, 2013.

Augsburger, David. *Dissident Discipleship: A Spirituality of Self-Surrender, Love of God, and Love of Neighbor.* Grand Rapids, MI: Baker, 2006.

Baden, Joel S. "The Violent Origin of the Levites: Text and Tradition." In *Levites and Priests in Biblical History and Tradition,* eds. Mark Leuchter and Jeremy M. Hutton, 103–116. Atlanta, GA: Society of Biblical Literature, 2011.

Barth, Karl. *Church Dogmatics* IV.3.2. Translated by Geoffrey W. Bromiley. Edinburgh: T and T Clark, 1962.

Bates, Matthew W. *The Gospel Precisely: Surprisingly Good News about Jesus Christ the King.* RENEW.org, 2020.

Beale, G. K. *The Temple and the Church's Mission: A Biblical Theology of the Dwelling Place of God.* Downers Grove, IL: InterVarsity Press, 2004.

Bergsma, John. *Jesus and the Old Testament Roots of the Priesthood.* Steubenville, OH: Emmaus Road Publishing, 2021.

Blenkinsopp, Joseph. *Sage, Prophet, Priest: Religious and Intellectual Leadership in Ancient Israel.* Louisville, KY: John Knox Press, 1995.

Bonhoeffer, Dietrich. *Ethics.* Dietrich Bonhoeffer Works 6. Minneapolis, MN: Fortress Press, 2005.

Brueggemann, Walter. *The Prophetic Imagination,* 2nd ed. Minneapolis, MN: Fortress Press, 2001.

Camp, Lee C. *Scandalous Witness: A Little Political Manifesto for Christians.* Grand Rapids, MI: Eerdmans, 2020.

Carter, Craig. *Rethinking Christ and Culture: A Post-Christendom Perspective.* Grand Rapids, MI: Brazos Press, 2007.

Chilton, Bruce. *The Herods: Murder, Politics, and the Art of Succession.* Minneapolis, MN: Fortress Press, 2021.

Cody, Aelred. *A History of the Old Testament Priesthood*. Analecta Biblica 35. Rome: Pontifical Biblical Institute, 1969.

Doak, Mary. *A Prophetic, Public Church: Witness to Hope Amid the Global Crises of the Twenty-First Century*. Collegeville, MN: Liturgical Press, 2020.

Dulles, Avery Cardinal. *Models of Church*, expanded ed. New York: Image Books, 2002.

Fitch, David E. *Faithful Presence: Seven Disciplines that Shape the Church for Mission*. Downers Grove, IL: InterVarsity Press, 2016.

Gilders, William K. *Blood Ritual in the Hebrew Bible*. Baltimore & London: Johns Hopkins University Press, 2004.

Greggs, Tom. *Dogmatic Ecclesiology*. Vol 1. *The Priestly Catholicity of the Church*. Grand Rapids, MI: Baker Academic, 2019.

Harmon, Matthew S. *The Servant of the Lord and His Servant People: Tracing a Biblical Theme Through the Canon*. Downers Grove, IL: InterVarsity Press, 2020.

Hauerwas, Stanley and Jonathan Tran. "A Sanctuary Politics: Being the Church in the Time of Trump." ABC Religion and Ethics, March 30, 2017, https://www.abc.net.au/religion/a-sanctuary-politics-being-the-church-in-the-time-of-trump/10095918.

Haydock, Nicholas. *The Theology of the Levitical Priesthood: Assisting God's People in Their Mission to the Nations*. Eugene, OR: Wipf & Stock, 2015.

Hicks, John Mark. *Come to the Table: Revisioning the Lord's Supper*. Abilene, TX: Leafwood Publishers, 2002.

Himmelfarb, Martha. *A Kingdom of Priests: Ancestry and Merit in Ancient Judaism*. Philadelphia: University of Pennsylvania, 2006.

Johnson, Luke Timothy. *Prophetic Jesus, Prophetic Church: The Challenge of Luke-Acts to Contemporary Christians*. Grand Rapids, MI: Eerdmans, 2011.

Kenneson, Philip D. *Life on the Vine: Cultivating the Fruit of the Spirit*. Downers Grove, IL: InterVarsity Press, 1999.

Lohfink, Gerhard. *Jesus and Community: The Social Dimension of Christian Faith*, translated by John P. Galvin. Philadelphia: Fortress, 1984.

_____. *No Irrelevant Jesus: On Jesus and the Church Today*, translated by Linda M. Maloney. Collegeville, MN: Liturgical Press, 2014.

Mason, Eric. *Woke Church: An Urgent Call for Christians in America to Confront Racism and Injustice*. Chicago: Moody Publishers, 2018.

McNeal, Reggie. *Kingdom Come: Why We Must Give up Our Obsession with Fixing the Church—and What We Should Do Instead*. Carol Stream, IL: Tyndale Publishers, 2015.

Nelson, Richard D. *Raising Up a Faithful Priest: Community and Priesthood in Biblical Theology*. Louisville, KY: Westminster/John Knox Press, 1993.

Niebuhr, H. Richard. *Christ and Culture*. New York: Harper & Row, 1951.

Nugent, John C. *Endangered Gospel: How Fixing the World Is Killing the Church*. Eugene, OR: Cascade Books, 2016.

_____. "End of Sacrifice: John Howard Yoder's Critique of Capital Punishment." In *Reading Scripture as Political Act: Essays on the Theopolitical Interpretation of the Bible*, eds. Matthew A. Tapai and Daniel Wade McClain, 287–304. Minneapolis, MN: Fortress Press, 2015.

_____. *Genesis 1–11*. The Polis Bible Commentary. La Vista, NE: Urban Loft Publishers, 2018.

_____. *The Fourfold Office of Christ: A New Typology for Relating Church and World*. Eugene, OR: Cascade Books, 2024.

_____. *The Politics of Yahweh: John Howard Yoder, the Old Testament, and the People of God*. Eugene, OR: Cascade Books, 2011.

Paas, Stefan. *Pilgrims and Priests: Christian Mission in a Post-Christian Society*. London: SCM Press, 2019.

Rooke, Deborah W. *Zadok's Heirs: The Role and Development of the High Priesthood in Ancient Israel*. Oxford: Oxford University Press, 2000.

Sheldon, Charles. *In His Steps: "What Would Jesus Do?"* Chicago: Advance Publishing, 1898.

Sheldon, Garrett W. *What Would Jesus Do?* Nashville, TN: Broadman & Holman Publishers, 1998.

Sider, Ronald J., Philip N. Olson, and Heidi Rolland Unruh. *Churches that Make a Difference: Reaching Your Community with Good News and Good Works*. Grand Rapids, MI: Baker Books, 2002.

Smith, Brittany and Natasha Smith. *Unplanned Grace: A Compassionate Conversation on Life and Choice*. Colorado Springs: David C. Cook, 2021.

Smith, C. Christopher. *How the Body of Christ Talks: Recovering the Practice of Conversation in the Church*. Grand Rapids, MI: Brazos, 2019.

Sorenson, Barbara DeGrote and David Allen. *Let the Servant Church Arise!* Minneapolis, MN: Augsburg Fortress Press, 2003.

Stassen, Glen H. et al, eds. *Authentic Transformation: A New Vision of Christ and Culture*. Nashville, TN: Abingdon Press, 1996.

Stott, John. *Issues Facing Christianity Today: New Perspectives on Social and Moral Dilemmas*. Basingstoke, UK: Marshall Pickering, 1984.

Streett, R. Alan. *Songs of Resistance: Challenging Caesar and Empire*. Eugene, OR: Cascade Books, 2022.

Thompson, James W. *The Church in Exile: God's Counterculture in a Non-Christian World*, rev. ed. Abilene, TX: Leafwood Publishers, 2010.

VanderKam, James C. *From Joshua to Caiaphas: High Priests after the Exile*. Minneapolis, MN: Fortress Press, 2004.

Volf, Miroslav. *A Public Faith: How Followers of Christ Should Serve the Common Good*. Grand Rapids, MI: Brazos, 2011.

Walton, John H. *Genesis*. NIV Application Commentary. Grand Rapids, MI: Eerdmans, 2001.

Webb, Stephen H. *Good Eating*. The Christian Practice of Everyday Life. Grand Rapids, MI: Brazos, 2001.

Wilson, Gerald Henry. *Editing of the Hebrew Psalter*. Society of Biblical Literature Dissertation Series. Chico, CA: Scholars, 1985.

_____. "The Shape of the Book of Psalms." *Interpretation* 46 (1992): 129–142.

Wright, N. T. *After You Believe: Why Christian Character Matters*. New York: Harper One, 2010.

Yoder, John H. *Discipleship as Political Responsibility*. Translated by Timothy J. Geddert. Scottdale, PA: Herald Press, 2003.

_____. *The Politics of Jesus: Vicit Agnus Noster*, 2nd ed. Grand Rapids: Eerdmans, 1994.

Index of Names and Subjects

Index of Biblical References